Nationalmuseum
Stockholm

Nationalmuseum
Stockholm

Scala Books

Contents

Foreword

Three years ago Stockholm's Nationalmuseum celebrated its bicentennial, making it one of Europe's oldest art museums and, like them, a child of the Enlightenment. The Nationalmuseum, whose current building was completed in 1866, also has connections with a larger family of European museums in its current architectonic form, because it was designed by the German architect Friedrich August Stüler, originator of the Neues Museum in Berlin, which in turn derived from Friedrich Schinkel's Altes Museum. The building now houses painting and sculpture made before 1900 – twentieth-century art moved to its own museum in 1958 – as well as one department for applied art and one for prints and drawings.

The selection of masterpieces in the Nationalmuseum described in this book barely touches the tip of the iceberg – the Department of Prints and Drawings, for example, has a collection numbering 800,000, making it one of the largest of its kind in Europe. Undoubtedly, one turns to the Nationalmuseum to see the most and the best of Swedish art; when it comes to foreign material, seventeenth-century Dutch and eighteenth-century French painting are well represented. Among the museum's specialities are collections of more than 300 icons and 4,500 European miniatures.

With this book spearheading the collection, we wish our visitors welcome to the Nationalmuseum in Stockholm.

Olle Granath
Director

The History and Collections of the Nationalmuseum

chapter 1

The Nationalmuseum has its roots in the old royal Swedish collections. Gustav Vasa, Sweden's first Renaissance prince, had a modest collection which was catalogued for the first time in 1529. It consisted of thirteen paintings that were kept at Gripsholm, a residence which was expanded and fortified into a fortress and castle during the 1530s and 1540s. In 1547 a new inventory was taken, by which time the collection had grown to 92 works. Even if its descriptions are brief, one can identify some works in it that today belong to the Nationalmuseum: *Crucifixion* by Cornelis Engebrechtsz, and *Lucretia* by Lucas Cranach.

The major acquisitions, however, were added during the first half of the seventeenth century and consisted primarily of war booty taken during the various Swedish campaigns in Germany. In 1631 Gustav II Adolf allowed Matthias Grünewald's triptych altarpiece to be dismantled and removed from the cathedral in Mainz; however, it was wrecked during its transport to Sweden over the Baltic Sea. Most importantly, a great many works from the Munich Art Gallery were brought to Sweden in 1632. The greatest prize was acquired with the conquest of Prague in 1648, when no fewer than 470 paintings were carried off to Stockholm. It was a short-lived victory, however, since the young Queen Kristina gave away some of the most significant northern European works: Dürer's paintings *Adam* and *Eve* to the king of Spain, and Holbein's *The Source of Life* to the king of Portugal. When she abdicated in 1654, she took with her most of the Italian art, which later adorned her residence in the Palazzo Riario in Rome. Of those works that remained in Stockholm, the bulk was destroyed in 1697 during a fire that ravaged Stockholm's medieval castle. Today, there are fewer than 30 paintings in the Nationalmuseum collection remaining from these spoils of war. They consist primarily of Netherlandish Mannerists such as Jan Massys, Frans Floris, Joachim Beuckelaer and Pieter Aertsen.

Kristina was succeeded by her cousin Karl X Gustav, who continued the conquests – and the art acquisitions – initiated by Gustav II Adolf. It was above all the campaigns in Denmark and Poland that produced results. Danish palaces were practically stripped bare in the Swedes' rampage. Karl X Gustav died in 1660 and it was his 24-year-old widow Hedvig Eleonora who established herself as the chief exponent of culture and patron of the arts during the minority of the crown prince. She became most interested in portraits that could be used to embellish the royal palaces she erected, including Drottningholm, the residence of the current royal family.

Her grandson Karl XII, who ruled Sweden during the first years of the eighteenth century, was better known for his martial deeds than for his contributions to culture, and it was not until the so-called Age of Freedom that art collecting resumed in Sweden. It then took several directions. Not only did King Adolf Fredrik and his energetic queen Lovisa Ulrika collect art, but a number of immigrants from the Netherlands (families such as De Geer, Grill, Sack and Peill) brought significant collections from their homeland. Count Carl Gustav Tessin (1695–1770) and Gustav Adolf Sparre (1746–94) were

B. Gagneraux, *Pope Pius VI Showing Gustav III the Vatican Sculpture Gallery*. Painting executed in Rome in 1785 at the request of Gustav III. Nationalmuseum (NM 829)

both passionate collectors, especially of French painting. As a young man during his Grand Tour of Europe (1714–19), Tessin become acquainted with the French painter Antoine Watteau, although at the time he lacked the resources to acquire anything more than some examples of his red crayon drawings. Tessin returned to France in 1728 and then had the opportunity to purchase works by contemporary artists with whom he was acquainted, such as François Lemoine, Noël-Nicolas Coypel, Nicolas Lancret and Jean-Baptiste Pater. In 1736 he made a brief visit to Venice, mostly to find artists to paint the ceilings of the new royal palace that was being built in Stockholm after the fire. He was impressed by Giovanni Battista Tiepolo and tried for some time to entice him to Stockholm. In the end Tiepolo declined, but Tessin brought back a number of his oil sketches, along with work by other Venetians, to give the Swedish rulers an indication of his intentions.

Tessin's greatest contribution as a collector was made during the years 1739–42 when he was living in Paris as Swedish ambassador to France. In addition to expressing his own passion for art, collecting for Tessin had both social and political dimensions: he had married into a wealthy family, and was thought to have unlimited resources. Boucher and Chardin, above all, became the objects of his interest, but he also acquired a great number of significant seventeenth-century Dutch paintings which were then fashionable in the French capital. He owned works by Rembrandt as well as by Ruisdael, Wouwerman and Teniers.

Tessin's passion for collecting became his undoing. In 1749 economic conditions forced him to sell all his paintings, as well as a very substantial number of drawings which he had largely acquired during his years in Paris. These works of art were purchased with private funds by King Fredrik I, who was not noted for his cultural investments. He immediately presented them to Crown Princess Lovisa Ulrika.

King Gustav III, who succeeded his father Adolf Fredrik in 1771, had strong cultural interests. His first acquisitions were important works belonging to his father and, in 1777, when his mother encountered financial difficulties, these were followed by her

P. Hilleström, *Interior of the Gallery of the Muses in the Royal Museum in the Palace, Stockholm*. Painted 1796. Nationalmuseum (NM 965)

entire collection. In 1779 he added 24 paintings from the Sack family of Bergshammar, a collection particularly strong in Dutch painting, including works by Rembrandt and his school. Gustav III made his purchases with public funds, expressly with the intention that his collection would become state property. He may have been motivated by a desire to avoid the humiliating way in which both of his parents' art collections were disposed. In 1780 he put on a display in a couple of rooms in the Royal Palace. Consisting primarily of Dutch paintings, it was open to a limited public. The major work was Rembrandt's *The Oath of the Batavians to Claudius Civilis*. This had attracted his attention when it was exhibited at the Academy of Art, as a loan by its then owner, Henrik Wilhelm Peill. Peill's widow later donated it to the Academy, which in turn deposited it with the Nationalmuseum.

In the winter of 1783–84 Gustav III travelled to Italy, officially for health reasons, but in reality to study the country's art. The great museums became special objects of his interest. During his month-long stay in Florence, he visited the Uffizi Gallery fifteen times. In Rome, he often went to the newly opened Museo Pio-Clementino; the best known of these visits was on New Year's Day 1784 under the personal guidance of the Pope.

Gustav III was captivated by the art from antiquity that he encountered in Rome, Naples, Pompeii and Paestum. His objective of creating a royal museum in Stockholm then took a new direction, and he resolved to complement his existing collection with antiquities. In Rome, practically anything a buyer wanted could be produced from fragments of antique sculpture; the artist Giovanni Volpato supplied the King with a complete set of Apollo and the nine Muses, based upon the series in the Vatican. The highlight of the King's collection was the sculpture *Endymion*, supposedly excavated

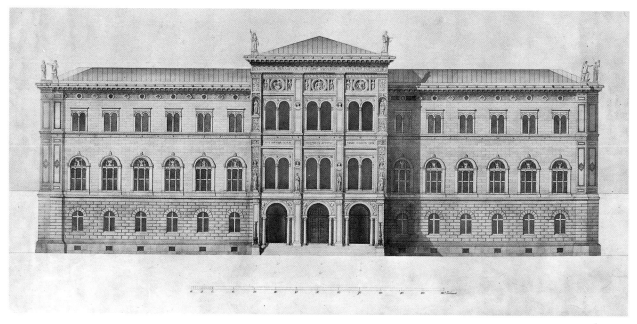

F. A. Stüler, *Final Proposal for the Nationalmuseum's Main Façade*. Ink drawing with watercolour. Nationalmuseum (NMH A70/1975)

with works by the Swedish Neoclassical sculptor Johan Tobias Sergel. The paintings consisted of approximately 200 works; for the most part the collection remained unchanged up until Gustav III's death in 1792.

From this point, it was a short step to a public museum. On 28 June 1792 the Royal Museum was founded as a memorial to the dead king, and the museum's first director, Carl Fredrik Fredenheim (1741–1803), immediately began to arrange new exhibition rooms within the palace which had direct access from the outside. In 1794, the museum was finally opened to the public. Fredenheim arranged and catalogued the collections, and made great efforts to supplement them. One obvious gap was the lack of Italian painting. Through Lars Grandel, a Swedish artist active in Italy, Fredenheim obtained information in 1796 about a private collection that belonged to a professor in Rome called Nicola Martelli. According to reports, it contained works by practically every significant Italian painter. Fredenheim trusted his informant, and purchased the collection sight unseen. It was fortunate for Fredenheim that he did not live to see the paintings, which arrived in Stockholm only in 1803, after a delay of several years. Works that had been proudly attributed to Masaccio, Leonardo, Raphael, Correggio, Giorgione, Titian, Veronese and Caravaggio turned out not to be authentic works by these masters, but third-rate paintings; with few exceptions they were relegated to the museum's storage rooms.

Fredenheim showed great personal interest in the antiquities, which were given appropriate exhibition space in one of the palace's wings. However, as time passed and the collections grew, this space proved inadequate. New works of art were brought to the museum, most of which had come from the Royal Palace. In 1844, the museum found an aggressive and energetic director in Michael Gustaf Anckarsvärd. Consequently, in May 1845 the parliament voted to allocate public funds for the construction of a new museum. From the very beginning the concept of a 'National Museum' was launched, probably to emphasise that representatives of the people were now taking over responsibility for the museum and its collection. It was significant that they chose to erect the new building as a counterpart to the Royal Palace, on the opposite side of Stockholm's inner harbour. The assignment to design the building went to a young Swedish architect, Fredrik Wilhelm Scholander, who proved unable to manage the task. Instead, the commission was given to the famous German museum builder F. A. Stüler who, among other achievements, designed the Neues Museum in Berlin. In 1866, after twenty-years' work, the new museum opened to the public.

Staircase in the Nationalmuseum. Illustration from *Ny Illustrerad Tidning*, 1866.

The museum lacked sufficient resources for purchases; all acquisitions were the result of donations. Featured among the donors was M. von Wahrendorff with a collection consisting mainly of Dutch paintings, and Adriaen de Vries' splendid sculpture *Psyche Carried by Cupids*. King Karl XV donated Rubens' magnificent versions of Titian's *Bacchanal on Andros* and *Worship of Venus*, and his brother Oskar gave Judith Leysters' *Boy Playing the Flute*. The limited public funds that were available were now used primarily for acquisitions of contemporary Swedish art – a major factor in the museum's national status. In 1872 Karl XV, a painter himself who was extremely interested in artistic endeavours, bequeathed to the museum his own extensive and important collection of approximately 400 paintings by Scandinavian masters.

In 1880, for the first time, the museum obtained a qualified art historian, Gustaf Upmark, as its director. International art continued to be acquired relatively sporadically, however, and primarily as the result of chance. One such incident was the acquisition of Rembrandt's *The Apostle Peter* which, at the time it was purchased, commanded a relatively modest sum because it was regarded as a work by an unknown Italian master. Only later, when conservation work was done, were the signature and the

Upper staircase with sculptures by J. T. Sergel. In the background is Carl Larsson's monumental painting, *Gustav Vasa's March into Stockholm in 1523* (photograph dated 1954).

date of 1632 revealed. Upmark also had good contacts with contemporary artists in Sweden, and saw to it that they were well represented in the museum's collections. However, at the international level his taste was conservative, and this was also true of his successor, Ludvig Looström, who headed the museum from 1900 to 1915. The first Impressionist painting in the collection was a work by Édouard Manet, *Young Boy Peeling a Pear*, donated in 1896 by the Swedish artist Anders Zorn. It was several years before any more French paintings entered the collection. The next was Gauguin's *Landscape from Arles*, acquired in 1911. That year, the organisation 'Friends of the Museum' was founded, with Crown Prince Gustaf Adolf active as its president. Its orientation was not as conservative as the museum's administration, and during its first years a series of works by Degas, Renoir and Sisley were presented to the museum. The Friends continued to enrich the Impressionist collection during the following decade, and also procured other significant older works, such as Georges de La Tour's *Saint Jerome*.

In general, the Swedish collection generated the most interest during the 1910s, 1920s and 1930s. Through private initiatives, the museum received two especially significant donations that greatly increased the breadth of the collection – European portrait miniatures from Hjalmar Wicander in 1927, and a collection of icons, mainly Russian, from Olof Aschberg in 1933. Funds allotted for purchases were insignificant, and only rarely could the museum accumulate enough money to invest at the international level. One such purchase, enormously important, was El Greco's *Apostles Peter and Paul*, acquired in 1935. The outbreak of war then impeded international contacts, while at the same time the museum began to run out of space. In 1948 the museum received a Rembrandt from a Swedish-born American collector, Nils B. Hersloff – a work that is most likely to be his last painting, *Simeon in the Temple*.

In 1958 the museum's chief curator Otte Sköld was able to secure a separate building for twentieth-century art, and the Museum of Modern Art (Moderna Museet) emerged as an increasingly independent organisation. The Nationalmuseum could then concentrate on expanding its existing collections of Dutch and French art. During the tenure of Carl Nordenfalk, an internationally renowned medieval scholar who replaced Sköld, a systematic acquisitions policy was established. Nordenfalk's most important acquisition was Watteau's *The Love Lesson*, which became the final jewel of the museum's collection of eighteenth-century French painting. It once belonged to Fredrik the Great, brother of the Swedish queen, Lovisa Ulrika. The economic difficulties encountered in its acquisition were inordinate and the accompanying protests were many, but they did not hinder the work from being obtained as planned. Some years later, Nordenfalk was able to complete the French collection with an additional Watteau painting and a fresh study by Fragonard, *The Beautiful Servant Girl*. The late eighteenth-century collection was enriched during the 1980s with a pair of works by Hubert Robert, together with an important work by Jean-Baptiste Le Prince.

The expensive Watteau acquisition was actually an exception. Owing to the museum's extremely modest acquisitions budget (by international standards), it was forced to concentrate on areas where prices for various reasons were not so high. In this way, it obtained a pair of allegories by Goya, *Spain, Time and History* and *Poetry and the Poets*, radiant masterworks less commercially desirable because of their large formats.

In the 1970s the museum underwent great changes. Carl Nordenfalk left his position as Director in 1969 to accept a professorship in the United States, and was replaced by Bengt Dahlbäck. The museum's greatest patron for six decades, King Gustav VI Adolf, died in 1973, and in 1976 the old museum was reorganised with the creation of a new government authority, the National Art Museums (Statens Konstmuseer). In addition to the Nationalmuseum, this organisation consisted of the Museum of Modern Art and the Museum of Far Eastern Antiquities. In 1970, the Nationalmuseum received one of its major donations in modern times from Grace and Philip Sandblom. This included several masterpieces, among them works by Delacroix, Courbet, Cézanne and Picasso.

One area in which it proved advantageous for the museum to concentrate was seventeenth-century France. The museum had long owned works by Georges de La Tour, Poussin and Simon Vouet, and in 1975 it complemented this group with Claude Lorrain's *Landscape with Rebecca Taking Leave of Her Father*. A series of works by lesser-known artists came to the museum during the 1970s and 1980s: the *Vegetable Seller* attributed to Louise Moillon, and additional works by Gaspard Dughet and Philippe de Champaigne, as well as Sébastien Bourdon. These acquisitions greatly enhanced the museum's traditionally strong French collection.

During the last decade, the Dutch collection has been enriched in a similar fashion with works by Meindert Hobbema, Lucas van Valckenborch and David Teniers the Elder, many of which had previously belonged to old Swedish collections.

Görel Cavalli-Björkman

chapter 2　　　　**Sweden**

Swedish painting 1600–1900

Foreign artists had worked at the Swedish court ever since the time of Gustav Vasa; with few exceptions, however, their stays were temporary. Gradually, these sporadic imports of foreign painters were replaced by a home-grown workshop tradition whose products found a market even outside the royal family. This led in turn to the creation in Stockholm in May 1622 of a large fraternal organisation based on the German model, the Portrait and Painter Office.

One of its first guildmasters was Jacob Heinrich Elbfas, born in Livonia. He had a large workshop and from 1634–40 was court painter to the Queen Dowager Maria Eleonora. Elbfas's portrait style is distinguished by a traditional, rigid figure pose. He remained guildmaster until his death in 1664, but could not withstand the onslaught of new artists who were summoned to the court at the beginning of Queen Kristina's reign.

The young queen certainly took great personal interest in the new orientation of the arts which came to characterise her time in power. In 1641 the Amsterdam engraver, Michel Le Blon, was assigned to act as her art agent, charged not only with purchasing desirable objects but also with recruiting artists. After six years, he succeeded in engaging the services of the Dutch painter David Beck, among others. Le Blon introduced not only high-quality art but also a new type of portrait – the allegorical portrait. Four other significant portrait painters quickly followed in Beck's footsteps: the two miniaturists Pierre Signac and Alexander Cooper, and the easel painters Hendrick Münnichhoven and Sébastien Bourdon (the last left Sweden after barely one year).

After Queen Kristina's abdication in 1654, a new generation of foreign artists was summoned to Sweden. Of these, the German David Klöcker (who took the name Ehrenstrahl when elevated to the nobility) gradually became the dominant artist. During a foreign study trip, Ehrenstrahl learned to paint in the pompous and allegorical Baroque style then reigning on the Continent. In spite of his conformity to its formulae, he had a talent for penetrating character depictions. While court painter, Ehrenstrahl concentrated upon portraits and allegorical compositions; he also painted animals, exotic fruits and national landscapes.

At the end of his life, Ehrenstrahl had competition from several French artists who were called to the Royal Palace in Stockholm. His own students contributed to the internationalisation of Swedish art. Michael Dahl and Christian Richter settled in London, as did Signac's apprentice Charles Boit.

The many years of war under Karl XII, and the years of famine that followed, did not have any appreciable impact on the situation of Swedish artists in the seventeenth and early eighteenth centuries. Georg Engelhart Schröder lived in Venice from 1709, where he became friends with Rosalba Carriera, among others. The latter, a highly regarded

David Klöcker Ehrenstrahl, *Black Cocks at Ground*, detail

Alexander Cooper
(London ca. 1605 –
Stockholm 1660)
*Count Magnus Gabriel De
la Gardie*
Signed
Watercolour on parchment,
6 × 4.9
NMB 2235

This portrait of the 23-year-
old count was probably
executed when he travelled
through Holland on the way
home after successfully com-
pleting ambassadorial duties
in France. The meeting may
have been the reason that
Cooper later came to
Stockholm. Transferred from
State Bank (Riksbank) collection in 1978.

**School of Jacob Heinrich
Elbfas**
Queen Kristina as a Child
Oil on canvas, 130.5 × 92.5
NM 6693

The unknown painters of this
portrait put great effort into
the overall impression and
the description of the beautiful costume. The characteri-
sation of the royal model, on
the other hand, is cold and
superficial. Purchased 1978.

Venetian miniature and pastel painter, eventually moved to Paris where, in 1720, she
became the teacher of another Swede in Paris, Gustaf Lundberg. Lundberg was one of
the first in a long line of Swedish artists who made their careers in Paris. He returned
home in 1745, but after seven years he left Sweden, and it was Alexander Roslin who
gradually became regarded as Lundberg's natural 'successor'. Roslin, like the miniature
painters Peter Adolf Hall and Niclas Lafrensen the Younger, became models of style in
contemporary French portrait painting.

Swedish art at home also experienced a kind of Golden Age. The arts were revitalised by
another round of French artists who were called up for the resumed construction of the
Royal Palace in Stockholm, beginning in 1732. Within portrait art, however, there was a
solid domestic tradition. The leading portrait painters included Lorens Pasch the
Younger, Per Krafft the Elder, and Carl Gustaf Pilo, who had returned to Sweden from
the Continent in 1772.

For a long time, sculpture was the most neglected category of art in Sweden. Swedish
sculptors made their start with Johan Tobias Sergel, who returned in 1779 after twelve
years of study on the Continent, primarily in Rome. Sergel had been educated in the
Rococo language of form, but in his development towards Neo-classicism his works

David Klöcker Ehrenstrahl
(Hamburg 1628 – Stockholm
1698)
Black Cocks at Ground
Signed, dated 1675
Oil on canvas, 283 × 270
NM 4862

One of the first landscape
paintings in Swedish art. The
artist recorded his subject
during the early morning
hours with a distant landscape in the background. In
this wilderness a face emer-
ges suddenly from the hut on
the right – did Ehrenstrahl
himself witness the ritual?
Transferred from Drottningholm Palace in 1951.

Pierre Signac
(Paris ca. 1623 – Stockholm
1684)
Queen Kristina
Enamel on gold, 5 × 3.7
NMB 2172

Signac's enamel does not
resemble any known larger
portrait, but was probably an
independent picture made
from life. This portrait of the
queen, showing her in an
imaginary costume, was most
likely executed during the
artist's first year in Stockholm.
Transferred from Royal
Treasury collection in 1978.

Hendrick Münnichhoven
(Utrecht, date unknown –
Stockholm 1664)
*Count Magnus Gabriel De
la Gardie and His Wife
Princess Maria Eufrosyne of
Pfalz-Zweibrücken*
Oil on canvas, 219 × 201
Grh 3426

This portrait is rich in sym-
bols which refer to Maria
Eufrosynes's condition. The
portrait belonged to De la
Gardie's collection in
Makalös Palace, Stockholm.
Bequeathed by Count Pontus
De la Gardie in 1973.

never degenerated into the frozen and idealised style that characterises much Neoclassical sculpture. There was always a substantial dose of warmth and sensuality in his
reverence for antiquity. With his return to Sweden, Sergel had hoped for a monumental
commission, but to his great disappointment he was forced primarily to execute portrait
busts and medallions.

Besides the traditional impact of French and Italian art, a clear English influence mani-
fested itself at the close of the Gustavian period. Carl Fredrik von Breda introduced
portraits by his teacher Joshua Reynolds and even those by Thomas Gainsborough,
while Elias Martin represented the English Watercolour style with its light, atmospheric
tones. After his second residence in England in 1788–91, Martin's landscape painting
was transformed. In his most visionary work – with contrasts between dramatic dark-
ness and supernatural light – he anticipated Romanticism.

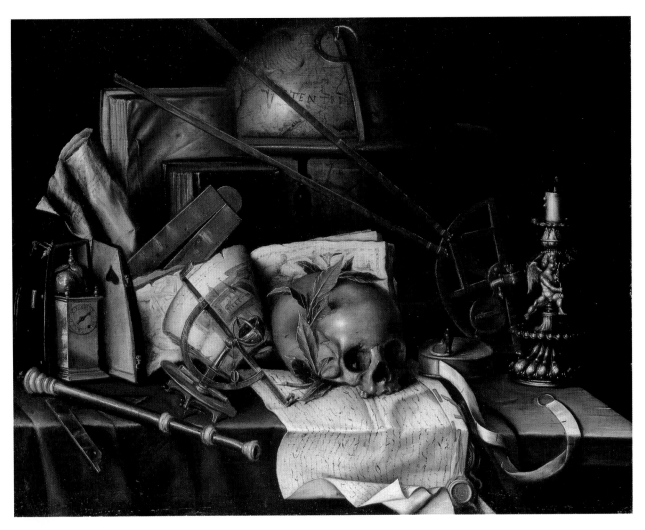

Christian Thum
(Stockholm ca. 1625 –
Stockholm 1696)
*Still Life with Astronomical
Instruments*
Signed
Oil on canvas, 68.5 × 84
NM 6871

Thum specialised in still life
painting. In this picture, one
of his most unusual, we find
typical symbols of mortality
– a skull, an hourglass and an
extinguished candle. Even
the scientific and musical
instruments symbolise the
transitional nature of everyday life. Purchased 1992.

The beginning of the nineteenth century was characterised by Romantic tendencies,
imported primarily from Germany, and to a certain extent from England. Carl Johan
Fahlcrantz was among the prominent landscape artists of the day, and historical painting was represented by Johan Gustaf Sandberg. The latter represents an important
trend within nineteenth-century Swedish culture, an era which drew inspiration from its
indigenous heritage, and from Old Norse literature and mythology. An interesting and
typical exponent of this trend in sculpture was Bengt Erland Fogelberg, whose larger-
than-life sculptures of the Asa gods Oden, Tor and Balder stood for many years in the
stairway of the Nationalmuseum.

During the first half of the nineteenth century Swedish painting embraced many com-
peting trends without a truly strong contribution by any one artist. Sweden had nothing
corresponding to the contemporary Danish Golden Age in painting. The year 1850,
however, showed signs of the beginning of a revitalisation. Triggering these developments was an exhibition that year in Sweden which revealed a new European artistic
centre previously unknown to the Swedes, namely Düsseldorf. It offered what seemed to
be a more timely approach to subject matter, with a somewhat greater element of
realism.

Those who went to Düsseldorf were primarily genre painters with an orientation towards
the depiction of Swedish peasant life. They included Bengt Nordenberg, Josef Wilhelm
Wallander and Kilian Zoll. Landscape painters were also attracted to Düsseldorf.
Among these was Marcus Larson, a landscape painter and student of the well-known
Andreas Achenbach. Carl d'Unker and August Jernberg were among those Swedes
specialising in depictions of contemporary German life. Historical painting, which still

Carl Gustaf Pilo
(Runtuna 1711 – Stockholm
1793)
Coronation of Gustav III
Dated 1782–93
Oil on canvas, 293 × 531
NM 1004

This coronation painting was
commissioned by Gustav III
in 1777, but was not begun
until 1782. The artist allows
his figures to blend into the
architecture of Stockholm's
Cathedral (Storkyrkan), in a
delicate mist of colour and
light. The painting, which
was never completed, was
intended as a pendant to
Ehrenstrahl's painting of
Karl XI's coronation. Transferred to the museum in
1865.

enjoyed a high status at the time, was practised by, among others, Johan Fredrik Höckert, Georg von Rosen and Gustaf Cederström. The latter's painting *Bringing Home the
Body of King Karl XII of Sweden* distinguishes itself as something of a national
treasure.

Around 1870, Paris again began to tempt young painters. It was there that the ideas were
born that would transform the whole of European art. The first Swede to adopt the new
landscape painting style championed by Camille Corot and the Barbizon school was
Alfred Wahlberg, who also attained a certain degree of success in Paris. The foremost of
the many Swedish landscape painters enticed to France by Wahlberg was Carl Fredrik
Hill. Hill was, to a large extent, isolated from his colleagues, with the exception of his
friendship with the German artist Max Liebermann. During the hectic years around
1875, Hill developed a type of painting which, with its intensity and technical daring,
must be counted among the most advanced of the epoch.

The Swedish painting of this period also found a person of similar significance in Ernst
Josephson. In his portraits and genre paintings Josephson was not as bold as Hill, but
there is the same strong engagement, the same probing artistic eye. Both also placed
high demands upon themselves – all too high, as both became afflicted by mental illness,
Hill in 1878 and Josephson ten years later. Both, however, continued their artistic work
after the outbreak of their illnesses, and their output from this period eventually played
a decisive role as a source of inspiration for an entire generation of Swedish artists.

Josephson provided the initiative for the so-called 'Opponents' – a group of artists,
dominated by those born in the 1850s, which opposed the outmoded instructional
methods at the Academy of Art. In the mid-1880s they formed the Artists' Association,
an influential organisation both at the end of the nineteenth and at the beginning of the
twentieth centuries. It gathered together the leading, more radical, artists of the day.
Most of its members had developed their styles while studying in France in the 1880s,
when many of them resided at the international artists' colony in the small village of
Grez-sur-Loing, south of Paris. Important Swedes such as Carl Larsson, Karl
Nordström, Bruno Liljefors, Nils Kreuger and Richard Bergh spent time there. The
author August Strindberg also visited Grez. He had worked for a short time during the
1870s as an art critic in his homeland and was a friend of many of the artists at Grez, but
was not really to turn to painting until after his visit to Grez.

Alexander Roslin
(Malmö 1718 – Paris 1793)
The Lady with the Veil
Signed, dated 1769
Oil on canvas, 65 × 54
NM 4098

The painting depicts the artist's 35-year-old wife, the French pastel painter Marie-Suzanne Giroust. This portrait, which is at the same time mysterious and elegant, has become a symbol of the eighteenth century in Sweden. It was originally part of the Österby collection. Gift made in 1945.

Alexander Roslin
Zoie Ghika, Moldavian Princess
Signed, dated 1777
Oil on canvas, 64.7 × 53
NM 6872

Roslin completed this portrait during his time as court painter in St Petersburg. This exotic beauty is painted in a white silk dress with silver embroidery, and with a coiffure crowned by a turban embellished with silver braids and roses. It was commissioned by Catherine II. Purchased 1991.

Anders Zorn pursued a path of study somewhat different from the other Swedes. French training was also significant for him, derived from Manet and the Impressionists above all, along with studies in London of the British water-colour tradition. Beyond Zorn's activities as an internationally renowned portraitist who also depicted Swedish life and nature, he was an outstanding etcher.

Towards the final years of the 1880s, the majority of these artists returned to Sweden. The French tonal painting and the blond palette which dominated in Grez were soon replaced by colours more suited to the Nordic light at dusk; details disappeared in favour of a synthetic simplification and monumentality. During the 1890s, the decade of National Romanticism, myths and folk tales returned to painting. Artists devoted themselves to a type of mood painting, with elements of Symbolism. They often chose the Swedish landscape as the bearer of these elements and to express the specific characteristics of various regions.

It was in this spirit that the nineteenth century concluded and the new century began. The palette soon brightened and elements of realism began to increase. But it would take almost a decade before a new generation of artists, also schooled in Paris, broke the Artists' Association's hegemony.

Magnus Olausson/Ulf Abel

Per Krafft the Elder
(Arboga 1724 – Stockholm
1793)
The Colstrup Sisters
Signed, dated 1754
Oil on canvas, 62 × 78
NM 2424

In his portrait of Birgethe
Dorte and Kirstne Mar-
garethe Colstrup, the artist is
still tied to the Rococo
palette of his teacher, Carl
Gustaf Pilo. Krafft is known
as one of Sweden's foremost
painters of children. Purchased 1924.

Pehr Hilleström
(Väddö 1732 – Stockholm
1816)
At the Embroidery Frame
Signed
Oil on panel, 39 × 33
NM 2452

Images of everyday life were
Hilleström's hallmark. In
this interior, one can discern
two women beside an
embroidery, which is
stretched out on a frame in
the candlelight. The back
wall provides an indication of
how paintings were hung at
the time. Bequeathed by
Rosalie Fraenckel in 1925.

Peter Adolf Hall
(Borås 1739 – Liège 1793)
Self Portrait
Dated ca. 1790
Watercolour and gouache on
ivory, 14.3 × 11.2
NMB 628

Hall initiated a revival in
miniature painting. His self
portrait is a virtuoso demon-
stration of almost impressionistic brushwork. Consul
Hjalmar Wicander purchased
it in 1920 from the artist's
descendants in Paris, later
donating it to the museum.
Gift made in 1927.

Elias Martin
(Stockholm 1739 –
Stockholm 1818)
*View from the Fersen Ter-
race, Stockholm*
Signed, dated ca. 1800
Gouache, 51 × 77.5
NMB 483

Here, the artist has faithfully
depicted the central part of
Stockholm, including the old
Makalös Palace (right foreground), the Opera House,
the partially completed
North Bridge, and a colourful assortment of ships in the
harbour in front of the Royal
Palace. Gift of J. P. Åhlén in
1925.

Johan Tobias Sergel
(Stockholm 1740 –
Stockholm 1814)
Amor and Psyche
Signed, dated 1787
Terracotta, height 73
NMSK 451

Sergel portrays the moment
when Amor leaves Psyche
because she defied the pro-
hibition against looking at
his face. In this final, full-
scale terracotta model, Sergel
subjugates drama in favour
of a harmonious formal
arrangement, in the spirit of
German aesthete J. J.
Winckelmann. Purchased
from the artist's estate in
1815.

Johan Tobias Sergel
The Faun
Signed, dated 1774
Marble, height 45, length 84
NMSK 357

In this pioneering work, Sergel demonstrated his consummate artistic skill. The final result was an almost living body, drunk with sensuality, which broke the decorum of Neo-classicism. Completed in Rome in 1774, it was later purchased by Gustav III. Acquired 1865.

Johan Tobias Sergel
A Rowdy Dinner
Wash drawing, 21 × 33.7
NMH610/1875

Sergel was not only a significant sculptor, but an important draughtsman. He rendered his figures here with violent frenzy and absolute precision. The artist himself is shown sitting on the near side of the table, surrounded by bottles. Purchased in 1875 from the artist's descendants.

Adolf Ulric Wertmüller
(Stockholm 1751 – Naamans
Creek, Wilmington, Dela-
ware 1811)
*Queen Marie Antoinette
Walking in the Trianon
Park with Two of Her
Children*
Signed, dated 1785
Oil on canvas, 276 × 194
NM 1032

This painting was commis-
sioned by Marie Antoinette
as a gift for Gustav III. Here
we see the queen with her
daughter, Marie-Thérèse-
Charlotte, and the first Dau-
phin, who died in 1789. In
the background is the
Temple of Love. The portrait
was reworked and sent to
Stockholm in 1786, where it
was presented to Gustav III.
Transferred in 1865.

Adolf Ulric Wertmüller
(Stockholm 1751 – Naamans
Creek, Wilmington, Dela-
ware 1811)
*Danaë and the Shower of
Gold*
Signed, dated 1787
Oil on canvas, 150 × 190
NM 1767

Wertmüller had originally
planned to sell the painting
to Catherine II of Russia, but
never received a response
from her. Instead, the painting accompanied the artist on
his trip to the United States
in 1798. In 1806 it was widely
exhibited, and brought
Wertmüller a substantial sum
in admission fees. Gift of J.
E. Heaton of New Haven,
Connecticut in 1913.

Carl Fredrik von Breda
(Stockholm 1759 –
Stockholm 1818)
*Portrait of the Artist's
Father*
Signed, dated 1797
Oil on canvas, 127 × 102
NM 941

Here, the artist painted his
70-year-old father, the claims
adjuster, Lucas von Breda.
The impressionistic brushstrokes and atmospheric
unity of model and back-
ground are typical of his
style. When the painting was
purchased by the museum,
the sitter was mistakenly
thought to be Sir Joshua
Reynolds. Purchased 1854.

Kilian Zoll
(Hyllie, Skåne 1818 –
Stjärnarp, Halland 1860)
*Midsummer Dance at
Rättvik*
Oil on canvas, 31 × 41
NM 2428

Zoll probably executed this
image of midsummer festivi-
ties – a theme that recurs in
Swedish art – using sketches
made from life while at
Dalarna in 1852, the year
before his arrival in Düsseldorf. The painting antici-
pates later developments,
both in its realistic attitude
and in its free brushwork.
Gift of Hugo Hjelmar in
1924.

Marcus Larson
(Lilla Örsätter, Östergötland
1825 – London 1864)
Waterfall in Småland
Signed, dated 1856
Oil on canvas, 190 × 233
NM 1713

Larson executed this work in
Paris, following the com-
pletion of his studies in
Düsseldorf. While it is based
upon on-the-spot studies of
his homeland, it also follows
the contemporary taste for
pictures of wild and
untouched nature. The painting can be interpreted as a
reflection of the artist's
Romantic nature; a form of
self portrait. Bequeathed by
Anna Wallenberg in 1910.

Johan Fredrik Höckert
(Jönköping 1826 – Gothen-
burg 1866)
*The Fire at the Royal
Palace, Stockholm, May 7th
1697*
Dated 1862–66
Oil on canvas, 214 × 284
NM 1355

The fateful fire that lay waste
to the old royal palace in
Stockholm is captured here
with convincing energy by
one of the greatest colourists
in Swedish art, who learned
his lessons from, among
others, the French Romantic
artist Eugène Delacroix. The
painting was completed
shortly before the artist's
untimely death. Gift made in
1883.

August Malmström
(Västra Ny, Östergötland
1829 – Stockholm 1901)
Dancing Fairies
Signed, dated 1866
Oil on canvas, 90 × 150
NM 1223

Romantic ideas about ani-
mate forces in nature are
commonly represented in
Swedish art beginning in the
late eighteenth century.
Here, the French-taught
Malmström reveals his debt
to the French Naturalist
Camille Corot, whose moody
landscapes Malmström
admired. Bequeathed by
Karl XV in 1872.

Gustaf Cederström
(Stockholm 1845 – 1933)
*Bringing home the Body of
King Karl XII of Sweden*
Signed, dated 1884
Oil on canvas, 265 × 371
NM 1363

This work has achieved its
position as an important history painting, not on account
of its authenticity, since
many things are incorrect,
but rather through its spirit
of lofty idealism combined

with its veracity, shown in
the artist's handling of the
uniforms. The painting is a
free replica of the original
version in the Gothenburg
Art Gallery. Purchased 1884.

Carl Fredrik Hill
(Lund 1849 – Lund 1911)
Landscape. Motif from Seine
Signed, dated 1877
Oil on canvas, 50 × 60
NM 1863

This work is among the most 'classical' of Hill's French landscapes, having its roots in 17th century tradition. At the same time, Hill's handling of colour and his brushwork are consistent with that of contemporary Impressionist painters. Hill's invitation, in 1877, to take part in the Impressionist Exhibition in Paris unfortunately was never taken up by the artist. Gift of the artist's sisters in 1915.

Carl Fredrik Hill
Waterfall with Stags
Pastel, 20.8 × 16.8
NMH 90/1926

Following the onset of mental illness in 1878, Hill's output consisted primarily of drawings, executed in a variety of media. His pictorial world often depicted mysterious, poetic visions. Here, two stags guard a roaring waterfall. Purchased 1926.

August Strindberg
(Stockholm 1849 –
Stockholm 1912)
The City
Dated 1903
Oil on canvas, 94.5 × 53
NM 4516

Strindberg, best known as
one of Sweden's leading
writers, devoted himself to
painting at several points in
his life. Despite the technical
and thematic limitations of
his painting (the majority of
his works are seascapes), his
canvases are profoundly
expressive. In this work,
there is the suggestion of a
mirage, close in conception
to his literary creations. Purchased 1949.

Ernst Josephson
(Stockholm 1851 –
Stockholm 1906)
The Water Sprite
Signed, dated 1882
Tempera on canvas,
144 × 114
NM 1905

The water sprite motif, with
its roots in Swedish folk
beliefs, plays a central role in
Josephson's work. This
romantic image reflects the
agony and ecstasy of creation, the artist's loneliness,
and his longing for atone-

ment. The same themes
occur in Josephson's poetry.
Purchased 1915.

Ernst Josephson
The Holy Sacrament
Signed
Oil on canvas, 127 × 76
NM 3602

The visionary tone in this painting is characteristic of the imagery of Josephson's work after 1888. His belief, at the time, that he was God's chosen One is expressed here by the resemblance between Christ's face and his own. This painting is an indication of how Josephson maintained his creative powers, despite his fragile mental state. Gift made in 1915.

Ernst Josephson
The Creation of Adam
Signed
India ink drawing, 38.5 × 24
NMH 38/1926

Many of the 2,000 or so drawings dating from Josephson's period of illness are considered to be masterworks of Swedish drawing. Here, the artist describes dynamically how God blew the spirit of life into Adam's body, with clear reference to Michelangelo. Purchased 1926.

Carl Larsson
(Stockholm 1853 – Falun
1919)
Autumn
Signed, dated 1884
Watercolour, 92 × 60
NMB 401

The backwards-facing figure
and the shredded letter in the
foreground are reminiscent
of Larsson's early style. The
dominant impression here,
however, is conveyed by the
soft tonalities and the feeling
that the painting was
executed from life.
Bequeathed in 1920 by
Herman Friedländer.

Carl Larsson
A Studio Idyll
Signed, dated 1885
Pastel, 66 × 50
NMB 191

This image, painted in Grez-sur-Loing, records the artist's wife, Karin, with their eldest daughter, Suzanne. It ranks among his greatest works, both as a portrait and as a genre painting. The Frans Hals reproduction in the background points to one of the artist's sources of inspiration. Gift of Pontus Fürstenberg in 1886.

Carl Larsson
Flowers on the Windowsill
Signed, 1890s
Watercolour, 32 × 43
NMB 268

The painting depicts one of the rooms in the artist's home in Sundborn, in the province of Dalarna. It was included in Larsson's album *A Home*, published in 1899, which had a major influence on Swedish interior design; the enormous success of the book reached far beyond Sweden's borders. Purchased 1900.

Karl Nordström
(Tjörn 1855 – Drottningholm
1923)
Storm Clouds
Signed, dated 1893
Oil on canvas, 72 × 80
NM 1893

As leader of the Artists'
Association, Nordström
occupied a central place in
Swedish cultural life. After
his time in France, the west
coast town of Varberg
became his artistic territory.
Its natural environment is
depicted here in a Synthetist
style that shows the influence
of, among others, the French
painter Paul Gauguin. Gift
made in 1915.

Christian Eriksson
(Taserud, Värmland 1858 –
Stockholm 1935)
The Same Johan Thuuri.
Portrait Head
Signed, dated 1911
Bronze, height 37
NMSK 1047

One of Eriksson's friends was
Hjalmar Lundbohm, founder
both of the town of Kiruna,
and its mining industry.
Through him, Eriksson met
the Same (Lapp), Johan
Thuuri, who recorded Same
life and legends. Eriksson
portrayed him both in a full
length statue, and in this portrait bust. Purchased 1912.

Nils Kreuger
(Kalmar 1858 – Stockholm 1930)
Evening on the Öland Plains
Signed, dated 1903
Oil on canvas, 65 × 183
NM 1879

For Kreuger, as for his friend Karl Nordström, exposure to the art of Gauguin and van Gogh in Copenhagen in 1892–93 was a decisive moment. One finds their influence in Kreuger's numerous paintings of the unique landscape on Öland, the island near his native town. Gift donated in 1915.

Bruno Liljefors
(Uppsala 1860 – Stockholm 1939)
Jays
Signed, dated 1886
Oil on canvas, 55 × 70
NM 6811

During the 1880s, Liljefors depicted the Swedish landscape with a precision based on deep familiarity – he was a hunter who enjoyed the outdoors. He often resorted to a micro perspective and focus on the foreground, the result of his interest in Japanese art and in photographic techniques. Gift of Friends of the Nationalmuseum in 1986.

Anders Zorn
(Mora 1860 – Mora 1920)
The Bride
Signed, dated 1886
Watercolour, 77 × 55
NMB 1928

During his first ten years as
an artist, Zorn devoted himself principally to water-
colours, often in a large
format. *The Bride*, a study in
greys, depicts his wife Emma
Lamm, and was painted in
Istanbul during their honey-
moon. Gift of Oscar and Lili
Lamm in 1967.

Anders Zorn
Omnibus I
Signed
Oil on canvas, 99.5 × 66
NM 6810

Zorn spent the winter of
1891–92 in Paris, concerning
himself with problems of
light and colour – the inter-
change between exterior and
interior, daylight and artifi-
cial light. Here, he addresses
them from the perspective of
a bus interior. His work
resulted in two paintings –
this one, and a variant,
Omnibus II which was
acquired by Isabella Stewart
Gardner of Boston. Pur-
chased 1985.

Anders Zorn
Midsummer Dance
Signed, dated 1897
Oil on canvas, 140 × 98
NM 1603

This painting has both an
Impressionist dimension,
with its interest in movement, dance and its loose
brushwork, as well as a
National Romantic dimen-
sion. This is evident here primarily in Zorn's focus on the
midsummer celebration with
its village costumes and
summer night light. Zorn
actively sought to preserve
Sweden's folk culture. Gift of
the Academy of Art, 1903.

Eugène Jansson
(Stockholm 1862 –
Stockholm 1915)
Riddarfjärden
Signed, dated 1898
Oil on canvas, 150 × 135
NM 1699

Jansson's subject is the view
from his studio in central
Stockholm. The landscape
has been transformed into an
interior mood painting, filled
with musical rhythm and
quiet melancholy. It also
reflects many of the ten-
dencies characteristic of
Swedish art in the 1890s.
Gift made in 1899.

Carl Wilhelmson
(Fiskebäckskil 1866 –
Gothenburg 1928)
Church-goers in a Boat
Signed, dated 1909
Oil on canvas, 185 × 196
NM 1796

The landscape and fishermen
of his native province of
Bohuslän are among Wil-
helmson's primary motifs.
Reserve and seriousness
characterise the church-
goers, who return in a rowing
boat after Sunday services.
Wilhelmson's style was strongly influenced by Synthetism
and Neo-impressionism. Purchased 1914.

Helmer Osslund
(Matfors, Medelpad 1866 –
Stockholm 1936)
Autumn
Signed, dated 1907
Oil on canvas, 116 × 202
NM 6371

Osslund was a native of the
northernmost part of
Sweden, and returned there
after his stay in Paris, where
he had studied for a short
time with Gauguin. This
monumental, stylised
description of the Swedish
mountains originally
belonged to a series of decorative paintings illustrating
the four seasons. Gift of
Friends of the National-
museum made in 1971.

chapter 3   # England and the USA

Engl.sh painting, like American and Canadian, is sparsely represented in the Nationalmuseum collection. Historically Sweden has had few connections with the Anglo-Saxon world, and the patterns of acquisition have mainly followed other paths.

The collection, which comprises approximately fifty works, concentrates on the eighteenth and nineteenth centuries. Several of the more interesting paintings joined the collection during the 1960s. These include *Maria, Lady Eardley* (NM 5893) by Thomas Gainsborough, a pair of portraits by Joshua Reynolds, and *Mrs Blade and Her Daughter* (NM 6178) by Gilbert Stuart.

Cecilia Engellau-Gullander

Thomas Gainsborough, *Maria, Lady Eardley*, detail

Peter Oliver
(London ca. 1594 – London 1647)
The Digby Family
Signed
Tempera on parchment,
15.5 × 24.6
NMB 969

Sir Kenelm Digby was an important figure in seventeenth-century England, active in diplomacy, science and navigation. He was also a close friend of the Dutch painter Anthony van Dyck to whom he gave commissions and whose group portrait of the Digby family was the model for this miniature. Donation from the Wicander collection, 1927.

Samuel Cooper
(London 1609 – London 1672)
Alice Bourne, Lady Digby
Tempera on playing card,
7 × 5.5
NMB 890

Alice Bourne married Lord John Digby, 3rd Earl of Bristol, in 1656. The museum owns a portrait of her husband, signed by Cooper and dated the same year. These two precisely rendered portraits may be the couple's wedding gifts to one another. She is depicted against a dark background without any embellishing effects. Donation from the Wicander collection, 1927.

Joshua Reynolds
(Plympton 1723 – London
1792)
Mrs Pigott of Chetwynd
Oil on canvas, 76 × 63.5
NM 5636

The portrait of Mrs Pigott is
not typical of Reynolds'
painting. As a rule, his portraits, with their models
taken from contemporary
London society, are more
splendid and idealised. This
image is simple and full of
character. Mrs Pigott's eyes
meet the viewer's unflinch-
ingly and directly. Her coun-
tenance matches her neatly
elegant attire. Purchased
1962.

Thomas Gainsborough
(Sudbury 1727 – London 1788)
Maria, Lady Eardley
(1743–94)
Dated 1766
Oil on canvas, 215 × 149
NM 5893

This portrait, executed in Bath, depicts the young beauty Maria Marow before her marriage to Sir Sampson Gideon, who was given the title of Lord Eardley in 1789. In his usual manner, Gains-

borough placed his model in an open landscape, with lush green vegetation framing the sitter. Gift of Friends of the Nationalmuseum in 1966.

Gilbert Stuart
(North Kingston 1755 –
Boston 1828)
*Mrs Blades and Her
Daughter*
Dated ca. 1785
Oil on canvas, 74 × 59
NM 6178

The model was a member of
contemporary London
society, and the portrait was
executed during the artist's
stay there in the early 1780s.
Like many of Stuart's portraits, this one is unfinished,
a fact that gives the viewer
the opportunity to study the
free brushwork and the
artist's technical skill. Purchased 1968.

chapter 4 France

The French collection at the Nationalmuseum is one of its most important. At its core is the work of contemporary artists collected by Carl Gustaf Tessin during several visits to Paris, beginning in 1728; many were purchased during his three-year employment as Swedish ambassador to France between 1739 and 1742. He bought works at the Salon exhibitions, but also visited artists in their studios and commissioned portraits of himself, his family and his dachshund. During his time as ambassador, he played a major role in Parisian cultural circles. Unfortunately, however, Tessin lived well above his means and in 1749, after his return to Sweden, he was forced to sell most of his collection. It was more or less on its way out of the country when it was purchased by King Fredrik I. Through Queen Lovisa Ulrika, it came into the hands of Gustav III, but he did not integrate it into his own collection in the Royal Palace, probably considering it too modern – the fashion at the time was for antiquity and seventeenth-century Dutch masters.

Today, Tessin's original collection which constitutes the core of the French collection is still more or less intact, and is in exceptional condition with most of the paintings in their original frames. This gives us a unique opportunity not only to study particular works, but also to experience how an art collection was amassed in the mid-eighteenth century. Tessin was a rapacious collector, with an extensive library, a significant number of prints, and an outstanding collection of master drawings that complement the paintings in important ways. Above all, he acquired important suites of drawings by Boucher, Chardin and other artists with whom he associated in Paris. These give us an extraordinarily rich picture of their artistic skills.

Later generations have, naturally, been tempted to work on, enlarge and supplement the collection and to extend it to include earlier and later works. It was natural to purchase an important painting by Watteau, *The Love Lesson*, when it became available in 1952, and to complement it a decade later with another work by this great Rococo artist, who had not previously been represented. Late eighteenth-century French art has been an area of particular interest, as shown by a series of purchases of works by Fragonard, Hubert Robert and others. At the time Sweden had a strong cultural orientation towards France.

Nineteenth-century French art was appreciated at the beginning of this century by Swedish collectors and gradually began to make its way into museums, above all through donations. A leader here was Crown Prince Gustav Adolf – later Gustav VI Adolf – along with the Friends of the Nationalmuseum. Anders Zorn gave the museum its first Impressionist painting, a Manet, in 1896 and, during the short directorship of painter Richard Bergh (1914–17), works by Cézanne, Gauguin, Renoir, Manet, Monet, Sisley and Matisse were added. In 1926, yet another great and wealthy enthusiast, Klas Fåhrµus, was forced to sell his collection, from which the Friends of the Nationalmuseum were able to salvage works by Renoir, Monet, Cézanne and Courbet, thereby enriching the museum's French holdings.

Jacques-André-Joseph Aved, *Count Carl Gustaf Tessin*, detail

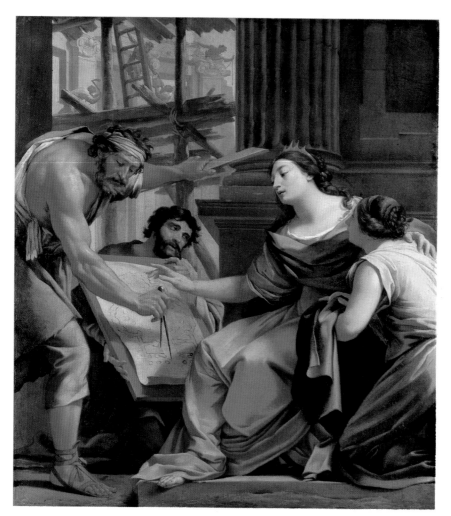

Simon Vouet
(Paris 1590 – Paris 1649)
*Queen Artemisia Building
the Mausoleum*
Dated ca. 1640
Oil on canvas, 161 × 139
NM 5179

Vouet painted this following
his return from Rome to
Paris, where he dominated
artistic life. The painting
records how the queen had a
large grave monument built
for her recently deceased
husband Mausolus in 352
BC. The work was probably
commissioned by Anna of
Austria after Ludvig XIII's
death in 1643. Purchased
1954.

Interest in seventeenth-century French painting has been less pronounced. In 1917, the
museum received Georges de La Tour's unique work *Saint Jerome* as a gift, which at the
time was thought to be a work by a Spanish artist. In 1928 Osvald Sirén presented a work
by the seventeenth-century master Nicolas Poussin, *Bacchus – Apollo*, the complicated
iconography of which later became the subject of great speculation. In 1974, the
museum acquired a work by Claude Lorrain, the last of the trio, *Landscape with
Rebecca Taking Leave of Her Father*, laying the basis for a broader representation of
French Baroque painting. Vouet, Bourdon and Philippe de Champaigne were already
represented, but in the 1980s additional works from this period by Claude Vignon,
François Nomé and Thomas Blanchet were added by Chief Curator Pontus Grate.

Except for works by the great masters, the art of the seventeenth century has not been
fully investigated by scholars. This is true above all for the entire realist tradition, with
the Le Nain brothers as foremost examples. However, almost all attributions in general
are still under discussion. The museum did not hesitate to acquire a particularly
interesting and high-quality work from this tradition in 1970, *The Vegetable Seller*,
occasionally attributed to Louise Moillon, and the recently purchased *The Concert*, both
of which were painted in the 1630s–40s.

Görel Cavalli-Björkman

Jacques Callot
(Nancy 1592 – Nancy 1635)
*The Temptation of Saint
Anthony*
Black crayon, pen drawing,
and wash, 44.8 × 67
NMH 2471/1863

This is a study for one of
Callot's most magnificent
etchings on the same subject,
dated a year before his death,
and executed in Nancy. In
his rendering, Callot brings
to life a horrific world reminiscent of Hieronymus
Bosch. Purchased from C. G.
Tessin in 1749.

Georges de La Tour
*(Vic-sur-Seille 1593 –
Lunéville 1652)*
Saint Jerome
Dated ca. 1623
Oil on canvas, 152 × 109
NM 2026

At first thought to be the
work of an anonymous
Spanish painter, the identity
of this work was not established until an exhibition in
Paris in 1934. De La Tour
was strongly influenced by
Caravaggio's dramatic light/
dark contrasts, but the painting is dominated by the tran-
quillity that is de La Tour's
hallmark. Gift of Friends of
the Nationalmuseum in 1917.

Claude Vignon
(Tours 1593 – Paris 1670)
*Moses with the Tablets of
the Law*
Oil on canvas, 160 × 131.5
NM 6820

Probably executed shortly
after the artist returned to
Paris from Italy, this painting was most likely commissioned by Huguenots who
placed great emphasis on the
Law of Moses. Purchased
1987.

Nicolas Poussin
(Les Andelys 1594 – Rome
1665)
Bacchus – Apollo
Dated ca. 1626–28
Oil on canvas, 98 × 73.5
NM 2669

This painting was the object
of a thorough investigation
by the renowned Erwin
Panofsky in 1960. He showed
that it had been completely
reworked, and drew attention
to the fact that the standing
male figure, originally Bacchus, had more assumed the
character of Apollo, protector of poets. Purchased 1928.

Unknown Artist
The Vegetable Seller
Probably 1630s–40s
Oil on canvas, 140 × 95
NM 6275

It has not been possible to
establish the author of this
painting, which is characterised by a realism similar to
that of the Le Nain brothers.
Purchased 1970.

Unknown Artist
The Concert
Probably 1630s–40s
Oil on canvas, 116 × 99
NM 6890

This painting belongs to the
strongly realistic and narra-
tive tradition that flourished
in France during the 1630s
and 1640s. As yet, there has
been no convincing attribu-
tion of this work to a particular artist. Purchased 1993.

Claude Lorrain
(Chamagne 1600 – Rome 1682)
Landscape with Rebecca Taking Leave of Her Father
Dated 1640–1641
Oil on canvas, 60.5 × 80
NM 6544

This is the fifty-second of the limited number of paintings the artist Claude Lorrain included in *Liber Veritatis*, where he listed his most important works. In this he stated that it was executed for one of Claude's most faithful clients, Angelo Giori, who was made a cardinal two years later. Purchased 1974.

Thomas Blanchet
(Paris 1614? – Lyon 1689)
Cleobis and Biton
Dated 1647–53
Oil on canvas, 88 × 130
NM 6780

This painting was probably executed during the artist's visit to Rome. It records Herodotus's story about Cleobis and Biton, who drove their mother, a priestess of Juno, to the temple in a cart. They were rewarded with 'the greatest gift the immortals can be given,' and fell asleep, never to awaken. Purchased 1984.

Sébastien Bourdon
(Montpellier 1616 – Paris
1671)
Queen Kristina of Sweden
Dated 1652–53
Oil on canvas, 72 × 58
NM 1072

Bourdon had worked in
Rome and was greatly influenced by Poussin, when he
was recalled to Sweden to be
court painter to Queen
Kristina. He stayed in
Stockholm for one year and
was mainly occupied with
portrait painting. Purchased
1869.

Antoine Coysevox
(Lyon 1640 – Paris 1720)
Portrait of a Man
Signed
Marble, height 56
NMSK 2239

Coysevox, the most impor-
tant French sculptor of his
day, executed large deco-
rative projects, as well as
more intimate subjects. It
has been suggested that this
is a portrait of the artist's
physician and friend Jean-
Baptiste Fermel'huis, who
cured him of a serious illness
in 1715. Gift of Friends of
the Nationalmuseum in 1978.

François Desportes
(Champigneulle 1661 – Paris 1743)
Silver Tureen with Peaches
Signed
Oil on canvas, 91 × 118
NM 800

Desportes, a still life specialist, was particularly influenced by Flemish still life painters. However, instead of their rich Baroque composition, he pursued a severe style, restrained in colour, in which he demonstrated an impressive virtuosity.
Acquired from C. G. Tessin in 1749.

Antoine Watteau
(Valenciennes 1684 –
Nogent-sur-Marne 1721)
The Love Lesson
Dated ca. 1716–17
Oil on panel, 55 × 61
NM 5015

Watteau's speciality was
painting fêtes galantes, such
as this one, showing young
people in playful relationships with erotic overtones.
This work, from his final
years, is painted on a coach
door, with underlying dec-
orations probably made by
Watteau. Purchased 1952.

Antoine Watteau
*Four Head Studies of a
Young Woman*
Black, red and white crayon,
34 × 24.5
NMH 2836/1836

Watteau made numerous
drawings like this, often
based on a model. He used
them several times as the
basis for figures in his
imaginative paintings.
Acquired from C. G. Tessin
in 1749.

Jean-Baptiste Oudry
(Paris 1686 – Beauvais 1755)
*The Dachshund Pehr with
Dead Game and a Rifle*
Signed, dated 1740
Oil on canvas, 135 × 109
NM 864

Oudry specialised in pictures
with hunting subjects and
also worked as a designer for
the royal tapestry workshops
in Beauvais and Gobelins.
This is a portrait of Tessin's
dog, Pehr, shown proudly
with his catch. Acquired
from C. G. Tessin in 1749.

Noël-Nicolas Coypel
(Paris 1690 – Paris 1734)
The Judgement of Paris
Signed, dated 1728
NM 793

Tessin purchased this painting during his visit to Paris in 1728. It exemplifies the Rococo style then dominating the salons of Paris. Purchased from C. G. Tessin in 1749.

Nicolas Lancret
(Paris 1690 – Paris 1743)
Binding the Ice Skate
Oil on canvas, 138 × 106
NM 845

While Lancret followed in Watteau's footsteps by recording fanciful situations, he was more accurate in his depiction of daily life among the French upper classes. Acquired from C. G. Tessin in 1749.

Jean Siméon Chardin
(Paris 1699 – Paris 1779)
*Still Life with Rabbit and
Copper Kettle*
Signed
Oil on canvas, 69 × 59
NM 785

Chardin was a proponent of
the middle-class tradition in
eighteenth-century French
painting. His still lifes are
unaffected, but characterised
by great sensuality, both in
the description of his motif
and in the treatment of colours, with their vibrant,
unmixed tones. Acquired
from C. G. Tessin in 1749.

Jean Siméon Chardin
The Draughtsman
Signed
Oil on panel, 19 × 17
NM 779

Chardin was able to instil
even the most mundane subjects with significance. He
recorded people resting and
in everyday situations without a hint of theatricality.
Acquired from King Adolf
Fredrik in 1771.

Jacques-André-Joseph Aved
(Douai 1702 – Paris 1766)
Portrait of Carl Gustaf Tessin
Oil on canvas, 149 × 116
NM 5535

This portrait was executed during Tessin's tenure as ambassador in Paris (1739–42). He is depicted in a private moment, as an art collector, in an open shirt and a dressing gown, and holds in his hands a print of Raphael's *Galatea*. Gift of the Tessin Society in 1960.

François Boucher
Study of a Rooster
Black, white and red crayon,
17.2 × 20.2
NMH 2953/1863

Tessin's collection of drawings included numerous
works by Boucher on a
variety of subjects. Among
them are unpretentious and
realistic studies of domesti-
cated animals such as this,
whose matter-of-fact presen-
tation are similar in spirit to
the works of Chardin.
Acquired from C. G. Tessin
in 1749.

François Boucher
(Paris 1703 – Paris 1770)
The Triumph of Venus
Signed, 1740
Oil on canvas, 130 × 162
NM 770

The highlight of the Tessin
collection, this is one of
Boucher's greatest works.
Painted in the Rococo style,
it celebrates female beauty
and eroticism. Tessin purchased the work directly
from the artist's studio.
Acquired from C. G. Tessin
in 1749.

Jean-Baptiste Perroneau
(Paris ca. 1715 – Amsterdam 1783)
Marquis de Marigny
Pastel on paper, 64 × 50
NMB 1986

Perroneau rendered this portrait in pastel crayons, a technique introduced to France by Rosalba Carriera. It was well suited to the Rococo demand for lightness and brilliance of colour. The sitter, who died in 1781, was the brother of Louis XV's mistress, Madame de Pompadour. Gift of Friends of the Nationalmuseum in 1969.

Jean-Honoré Fragonard
(Grasse 1732 – Paris 1806)
The Beautiful Servant Girl
Oil on canvas, 46 × 60.5
NM 5415

Fragonard's art frequently expresses the joy of life and sensuality. This is certainly the case here, where one sees his virtuosity as an artist in the rapid brushstrokes and colourful finesse. Purchased 1958.

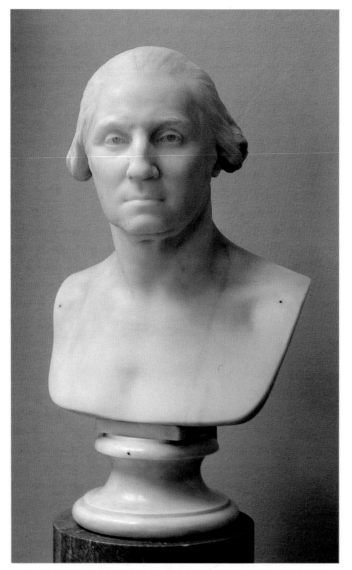

Antoine Houdon
(Versailles 1741 – Paris 1828)
George Washington
Dated ca. 1785
Marble, height 63
NMSK 1115

Houdon succeeded here in combining a Rococo liveliness with Neo-classicism's demand for clarity and restraint. In 1785, Houdon was invited to the United States in order to sculpt the president's portrait. There, he completed many portrait busts, of which this is probably one of the first. Gift of Hjalmar Linder in 1918.

Jacques-Louis David
(Paris 1748 – Brussels 1825)
Lictors Returning to Brutus the Bodies of his Sons
Sketch, oil on canvas, 28 × 35
NM 2683

The work of David, painter of the French Revolution, embodied a new morality. Lucius Junius Brutus established the Roman Republic in the sixth century BC, and had his two sons executed for treason. The painting is a sketch for the larger version in the Louvre, executed in 1789. Gift of John Johnson in 1928.

Théodore Géricault
(Rouen 1791 – Paris 1824)
The Severed Heads
Probably 1818
Oil on canvas, 50 × 61
NM 2113

Géricault was fond of recording death and dying: he studied terminally ill patients at hospitals and obtained the guillotined heads of criminals. This painting was a study for the *Raft of the Medusa* in the Louvre. Gift made in 1918.

Camille Corot
(Paris 1796 – Paris 1875)
Red Cliffs at Città Castellana
Dated 1826–27
Oil on canvas, 36 × 51
NM 2060

Corot, one of the nineteenth century's pioneers of outdoor landscape painting, completed this colourful and rich outdoor study while on an extended visit to Rome. Its tranquil, lyrical tone is typical of his style. Purchased 1917.

Eugène Delacroix
(Charenton-Saint-Maurice 1798 – Paris 1863)
Lion Hunt
Signed, dated 1855
Oil on canvas, 56.8 × 73.8
NM 6350

Delacroix was a leading figure of the Romantic movement in painting. He was particularly drawn to dramatic subjects, such as hunts, which he rendered in rich colours. Gift of Grace and Philip Sandblom 1970.

Gustave Courbet
(Ornans 1819 – La Tour de
Peilitz 1877)
Jo, the Beautiful Irish Girl
Signed, dated 1866
Oil on canvas, 54 × 65
NM 2543

Courbet painted this portrait
at a seaside resort in Nor-
mandy. He was attracted by
'the beauty of an extraordi-
nary red-headed woman
whom I have begun to paint.'
Jo was the mistress of the
American artist J. A. M.
Whistler, and Courbet made
no fewer than four versions
of this image. Gift of Friends
of the Nationalmuseum in
1926.

Jean-Baptiste Carpeaux
(Valenciennes 1827 –
Asnières 1875)
Antoine Watteau
1860s
Plaster with brown patina,
height 57
NMSK 2234

Like Watteau, Carpeaux was
born in Valenciennes, and he
planned to raise a monument
to the great Rococo painter
in their home town. Car-
peaux identified with his
townsman in many ways.
This portrait, which was a
part of Carpeaux's preparatory work for the monument,
bears a striking resemblance
to the sculptor himself.
Acquired in 1977.

Édouard Manet
(Paris 1832 – Paris 1883)
Young Boy Peeling a Pear
Probably 1868
Oil on canvas, 85 × 71
NM 1498

For Manet, the colourful possibilities of painting were paramount; the play of light and the harmony of tone were more important than any psychological considerations inherent in his subject. For this reason, he is often considered as a harbinger of Impressionism. Gift of Anders Zorn in 1896.

Paul Cézanne
(Aix-en-Provence 1839 –
Aix-en-Provence 1906)
Landscape
Signed, dated 1879–82
Oil on canvas, 73 × 92
NM 1999

It is above all in his landscapes that one senses the
geometric structure underlying most of Cézanne's pictures. Here one also finds the
subtle dialogue between
warm and cool colours that
typified his work. Gift of
Friends of the National-
museum in 1916.

Paul Cézanne
Still Life with Statuette
Dated ca. 1895
Oil on canvas, 63 × 81
NM 2545

In his painting, Cézanne
sought a balance between the
dynamic intensity of Impressionism and the old masters'
patience in constructing a
stable composition from a
continuous dialogue between
colour and form. The painting belonged to the collection
of Klas Fåhræus. Gift of
Friends of the National-
museum in 1926.

71

Alfred Sisley
(Paris 1839 – Moret-sur-Loing 1899)
On the Banks of the Loing
Signed, dated 1896
Oil on canvas, 54 × 65
NM 1770

Sisley, the French Impressionist of English parentage, was, along with Monet, the most consistent of the group. This painting is typical of his style, with its loose brushwork, avoidance of contours, and interest in light effects. Gift of Friends of the Nationalmuseum in 1913.

Claude Monet
(Paris 1840 – Giverny 1926)
Motif from the Schelde River Estuary
Signed, dated 1871–1872
Oil on canvas, 34 × 74
NM 2513

Returning from London to Paris in 1871, Monet stayed for a time in Holland, where this was executed. The painting, long considered a view from Schelde, depicts the confluence of the Voorzaam river and Ijccelmeer. Formerly the property of Klas Fåhræus. Gift of Friends of the Nationalmuseum in 1926.

Auguste Rodin
(Paris 1840 – Paris 1917)
Danaide
Dated ca. 1885
Terracotta, height 20
NMSK 1854

The museum's terracotta version of this sculpture is unique in this medium, although versions in marble and bronze are known. The subject, with its motif taken from the myth of King Danaus' daughters who were condemned to eternal labour for murdering their husbands, was intended as part of Rodin's famous *Gates of Hell*. Purchased 1964.

Auguste Renoir
(Limoges 1841 – Cagnes 1919)
Mother Anthony's Tavern
Signed, dated 1866
Oil on canvas, 149 × 131
NM 2544

Executed in 1866 in the village of Marlotte, near the Forest of Fontainebleau, this early work by Renoir still betrays the influence of Courbet. Here, he depicts several of his colleagues: Sisley is on the right, and beside him are Le Coeur and Monet. The painting belonged to Klas Fåhræus. Gift of Friends of the Nationalmuseum in 1926.

Auguste Renoir
La Grenouillère
Signed, dated 1868
Oil on canvas, 66 × 81
NM 2425

One of the key works of early Impressionism. In depicting this fashionable suburban resort, Renoir captured the glittering water, the flashes of sunlight and the movement of the strolling people. He made several paintings of *La Grenouillère*, as did his friend Monet, with whom he worked closely. Gift made in 1924.

Berthe Morisot
(Bourges 1841 – Paris 1895)
In the Bois de Boulogne
Dated 1879
Oil on canvas, 61 × 73.5
NM 5525

Morisot is one of the few women among the Impressionists, and her subject matter largely comprised women, children and female relationships. The painting is among her finest, with its lightness of tone. Gift of C.B. Nathorst in 1960.

Paul Gauguin
(Paris 1848 – Marquesa
Islands 1903)
Landscape from Brittany
Signed, dated 1889
Oil on canvas, 72 × 91
NM 2156

Gauguin moved to Brittany
for the second time in 1888,
when he became a central
figure in the Pont Aven
artists' colony. There, he
experimented with a new
formal, synthetic style, of
which this painting is an
early example. Formerly the
property of the artist and
Nationalmuseum director
Richard Bergh. Gift of
Hjalmar Granhult in 1919.

Pierre Bonnard
(Fontenay-aux-Roses 1867 –
Le Cannet 1947)
Umbrellas in the Snow
Signed, dated 1910
Oil on canvas, 60 × 65
NM 5969

Bonnard stands at the brink
of modern painting and represents, with his lyrical
impressions and colourful
sensibility, a synthesis of tradition and modernism in
French painting. Gift of Rolf
de Maré in 1966.

chapter **5** # Italy

The Nationalmuseum's collection of Italian painting is small and uneven, and contains relatively few masterpieces. Historically, Sweden had weak links with the Mediterranean world; she converted to Protestantism in the 1520s, thereafter alienating herself from southern European culture. The Italian paintings, primarily Venetian, that were brought to Stockholm in 1649 as a result of the Swedish army's sacking of Prague, stayed there only five years as Queen Kristina considered the collection to be her private property, and took it with her to Rome. The collection remained in Rome for several centuries; not even Gustav III reclaimed it during his 1783–84 visit to Italy. Although he had arranged the beginnings of a gallery in the Royal Palace, he had no intention of adding Italian painting. Instead, he focused on trying to acquire antique sculpture, inspired by the recent interest in antiquity resulting from the discovery and excavation of Pompeii, Herculaneum and Hadrian's Villa.

In addition to the interest in collecting Italian painting, there were lively contacts with the country in connection with the building of the new Royal Palace, begun in 1700. The architect, Nicodemus Tessin the Younger, was a great admirer of Roman architecture, and paraphrased it in the Royal Palace. When his son Carl Gustaf Tessin visited Venice in 1734, he made careful note of the artistic activities there, and brought home a small collection of sketches by the most famous Venetian painters, including Giovanni Battista Tiepolo and Canaletto. The majority of these were to end up in the Nationalmuseum via Royal collections.

Carl Gustaf Tessin also amassed an important collection of drawings that entered the Nationalmuseum, and among these are works by the Renaissance's greatest masters. Nonetheless, the Nationalmuseum collection still lacks examples of Italian Renaissance and Baroque painting. A first, but unfortunately unsuccessful, attempt to improve this situation was made through the acquisition of the Martelli collection by Fredenheim in 1804. From this the Nationalmuseum gained a single Italian Baroque painting, Giovanni Battista Recco's *Still Life with Fish and Oysters*. A new attempt was made in 1852, when several paintings from Johan Niklas Byström's collection were acquired. Byström, a Swedish sculptor, lived like a prince in Rome and owned approximately 300 paintings. When he died in 1848, the Nationalmuseum attempted to purchase all of them; only thirty works were acquired, and most of these were optimistically misattributed. Only one work from the Byström collection, a Bronzino portrait, merits discussion here.

For many years, the museum was guided by the exceptional expertise of Osvald Sirén, one of the greatest experts on Italian art, particularly the early Renaissance. He worked at the Nationalmuseum first from 1900 to 1907, but returned in 1926 after a period as professor at Stockholm University and stayed until 1942. Strangely enough, he did not play a decisive role in museum acquisitions, and the only significant Italian painting acquired with his initiative was Perugino's *Saint Sebastian*.

Domenico Ghirlandaio, *Head of an Old Man*, cut

Bartolomeo della Gatta
(ca. 1450–1500, places
unknown)
Nativity
Dated ca. 1485
Gouache on parchment,
15.3 × 28
NMB 1801

This miniature belonged to a
prayer book, *Missale ad
usum Capellae Sixtinae*,
commissioned by Pope
Sixtus IV for the Sistine
Chapel. It was part of the
richly ornamented first page
to the antiphon of the Christ-
mas mass. The book was
taken by Napoleon's soldiers
in 1798, broken up, and sold
in 1825. Acquired 1960.

Francesco Laurana
(attributed)
(La Vrana, Dalmatia 1420/30
– Avignon 1502)
*Portrait Bust of a Young
Sicilian Nobleman*
Marble, 51.5
NMSK 2132

It is clear that this charac-
terful portrait records the
visage of a nobleman, due to
its identifiable hat and wide
gold chain. The bust comes
from an old, princely collection in Palermo. Laurana
worked in Sicily from 1466 to
1471. Gift of Friends of the
Nationalmuseum in 1972.

Giovanni Bellini
(Venice ca. 1430 – Venice
1516)
Christ Crowned with Thorns
Dated ca. 1515–16
Oil on panel, 107 × 70
NM 1726

This gripping painting of a
theme to which Bellini often
returned is considered
among the artist's last works.
It is thought that he may
have intended it to decorate
his own grave monument.
The painting was damaged in
a fire at an early stage and
has recently undergone a
thorough conservation.
Acquired 1911.

Domenico Ghirlandaio
(Florence 1449 – Florence
1494)
Head of an Old Man
Silverpoint pen drawing,
heightened with white,
28.2 × 21.4
NMH 1/1863

This was a preparatory study
for a painting (now in the
Louvre) of an old man and
his grandson. The costly
frame is the work of Giorgio
Vasari, in whose collection
this drawing once belonged.
Acquired from C. G. Tessin
in 1749.

The few attempts made since at building an Italian Renaissance collection, similarly
have not been particularly successful. In recent years, the prices for works of this type
have risen to such heights that the Nationalmuseum, like most public institutions with
limited resources, is completely excluded from the market. A final chance presented
itself during the 1950s, when the museum declined the opportunity to acquire Titian's
magnificent late work, *Allegory of Time Guided by Wisdom* (now in the National
Gallery, London). We have, however, added to the eighteenth-century Venetian collection, which already contained several significant works; Francesco Guardi's picture of
the Piazza San Marco, acquired in 1964, filled an important gap.

Görel Cavalli-Björkman

Pietro Perugino
(Città della Pieve, ca. 1450 –
Fontignano 1523)
Saint Sebastian
Signed, dated 1500
Oil on panel, 174 × 88
NM 2703

Perugino probably painted
this, one of his few signed
works, when he was a pupil
in Raphael's studio. Gift of
Friends of the National-
museum in 1928.

Raphael
(Urbino 1483 – Rome 1520)
Adoration of the Kings
Dated ca. 1503
Brown pencil over
silverpoint, 27.2 × 42
NMH 296/1863

This drawing is the final
study for one of the predella
panels of Raphael's *Corona-tion of the Virgin*, completed
in 1503 for the church of San
Francesco in Perugia; the
painting has been in the Vati-can collection since 1817.
Acquired from C. G. Tessin
in 1749.

Dosso Dossi
(Mantua? 1489/90 – Ferrara
1542)
*Portrait of a Man in a Black
Beret*
Oil on canvas, 85.5 × 71
NM 2163

This painting was acquired
by Queen Kristina in Rome,
and is an example of her
strong interest in Venetian
art. For many years,
Romanino was considered
the artist, but it has now
been firmly attributed to
Dossi, who was clearly influ-enced here by Raphael and
Titian. Gift of Hjalmar
Linder in 1919.

Agnolo Bronzino (attributed)
(Monticelli 1503 – Florence
1572)
*Portrait of Isabella di
Medici*
Oil on panel, 44 × 36
NM 37

This painting manifests the
psychological insight typical
of Florentine Mannerism.
Purchased from the J. N.
Byström collection in 1852.

Giovanni da Bologna
(workshop of)
(Douai 1524 – Florence 1608)
Neptune
Bronze, height 115
NMSK 351

Giovanni da Bologna,
Flemish by birth, worked
primarily in Florence. He
executed monumental sculptures in bronze and marble,
as well as smaller works for
private collectors. His
stylistic attributes include
a virtuoso technical ability
and outstanding command
of the form's energetic pose.
Purchased 1771.

Giovanni Battista Recco
(Naples 1615? – Naples
1660?)
*Still Life with Fish and
Oysters*
Signed, dated 1653
Oil on canvas, 100 × 126
NM 759

Still life painting developed
during the sixteenth century
primarily in Spain and in the
Spanish colony of Naples.
This painting, signed GBR,
was for many years misattributed to the Neapolitan
school's foremost still life
artist, Giovanni Battista
Ruoppolo. Purchased from
Nicola Martelli in 1804.

Bernando Cavallino
(Naples 1616 – Naples 1656)
*Judith with the Head of
Holofernes*
Signed
Oil on canvas, 118 × 94
NM 80

Cavallino was a native
Neapolitan, whose work
gradually developed a dramatic naturalistic style. This
was first introduced to
Naples by the Roman painter
Caravaggio, who worked
there from 1606 to 1609. His
style was well suited to
bloody subjects from the Old
Testament, and to the history
of the martyrs. Gift of Karl
XV of Sweden in 1864.

Pietro Balestra
(Siena mid-17th century –
Rome after 1729)
Cardinal Decio Azzolino
Dated ca. 1660
Marble, height 104
NMSK 1455

This portrait, which
remained in the sitter's
family until the 1920s, has
traditionally been attributed
to Bernini. Recent docu-
mentation, however, has
proved that the portrait was
executed by his pupil
Balestra, who was employed
by Queen Kristina. Gift of
Friends of the National-
museum in 1940.

Giovanni Battista Tiepolo
(Venice 1696 – Madrid 1770)
The Generosity of Scipio
Dated ca. 1743
Oil on canvas, 60 × 44
NM 191

Tiepolo was a renowned
painter of decorative frescoes
who worked in different parts
of Europe. This is a preparatory study for one of his frescoes in the Villa Cordelina,
outside Vicenza. How this
painting arrived in Sweden is
unknown. Purchased from
King Adolf Fredrik in 1771.

Michele Giovanni Marieschi
(Venice 1710 – Venice 1743)
*Staircase in a Renaissance
Palace*
Oil on canvas, 36 × 55 NM 50

Marieschi's architectural fan-
tasies would be inconceivable
without the precedent of
Piranesi. Like him, Marieschi
is interested in the play of

light and the modulation of
colours in an enclosed and
mysterious architectural
world. Purchased from
Gustav III in 1792.

Antonio Canaletto
(Venice 1697 – Venice 1768)
View of the Grand Canal in Venice
Oil on canvas, 101 × 162
NM 49

Canaletto specialised in recording the piazzas of Venice and views of the Grand Canal in paintings that were detailed and exact. At the same time, he con- veyed the intense mood of the city produced by its char- acteristic lighting effects. Purchased from Gustav III in 1792.

Francesco Guardi
(Venice 1712 – Venice 1792)
Piazza San Marco, Venice
Signed
Oil on canvas, 50 × 85
NM 5830

The painting, one of Guardi's early works, represents a classic theme in his oeuvre. Here, the artist chose to record the entire Piazza through the use of an exag- gerated perspective. Pur- chased 1964.

The Netherlands, Flanders and Holland

chapter 6

From the late middle ages, Sweden's artistic contacts were directed largely towards Germany and The Netherlands. Many Swedish churches were embellished with Netherlandish altarpieces, especially during the fifteenth century. These have been largely preserved as Protestantism spread quietly through Sweden without any trace of iconoclasm. One of the earliest foreign artists working in Sweden was Lambert Ryckx of Antwerp, who worked for the crown in the mid-sixteenth century. Gustav Vasa's collection at Gripsholm Castle was dominated by Netherlandish as well as German painting. Even today, the Nationalmuseum owns a *Crucifixion* by Cornelius Engebrechtsz (NM 264) and *Adoration of the Kings* (NM 533), which can be traced to the Gripsholm collection.

The sacking of Prague in 1649 brought hundreds of Netherlandish paintings to Sweden: some entered the Royal collection, while others were kept by triumphant military leaders. The majority of these Netherlandish paintings remained in the Royal Palace when Queen Kristina abdicated, but their numbers were greatly reduced through royal gifts, and the Palace fire in 1697. Paintings such as Frans Floris' *The Elder's Feast of the Sea Gods*, and Jan Massys' *Venus Cythereia* can be traced via the Royal collections to Prague during the time of Rudolph II. This is also the case for Jan van Hemessen's *Virgin and Child* and Adriaen de Vries' *Psyche Carried by Cupids*. These two paintings were removed from the Royal collection at some point, but were later donated to the museum. Even today, paintings that can be traced to the sack of Prague emerge in private collections, and on more than one occasion the Nationalmuseum has been able to acquire them.

Another wave of Netherlandish painting came to Sweden with a group of wealthy Dutch families, who settled in the country at the end of the seventeenth century. They brought their heirlooms with them, and in this way several important Rembrandts arrived in Sweden, eventually finding their way to the Nationalmuseum. *The Apostle Peter* was brought by the von Cracow family; *The Kitchen Maid* by the Sack family; and *The Oath of the Batavians to Cladius Civilis* by the Peill family.

During the eighteenth century, Netherlandish art was very much in fashion in Paris, which is reflected in the paintings which originate from the royal collections of Adolf Fredrik and Lovisa Ulrika, and C. G. Tessin. Among the works originally in Lovisa Ulrika's collection are: Rubens' *Susannah and the Elders*, Pieter de Hooch's *Interior with Young Lady Reading*, from Adolf Fredrik, Van Dyck's *Saint Jerome*, and Jan van de Cappelles' *Harbour Scene with Reflecting Water*. Tessin was particularly interested in landscape (he purchased Ruisdael's *View of Egmont*), but he also bought the remarkable painting *Sleeping Student* by the little-known artist Constantin Verhout, as well as an early female portrait by Rembrandt. Gustav III too bought several Netherlandish paintings, principally adding to the Royal Palace's collection with works by Netherlandish artists.

Rembrandt, *The Oath of the Batavians to Claudius Civilis*, detail

Dirk Bouts
(Haarlem ca. 1420 – Löwen
1475)
Head of Christ
Dated 1468
Oil on panel, 22.5 × 19
NM 6632

This painting is probably a
fragment of an altarpiece
depicting the *Last Judgement*, which the artist was
commissioned to paint for
the city hall of Louvain in
1468. The two wings of the
altarpiece are now in the
Musée des Beaux-Arts in
Lille, and in the Louvre; the
centre panel is lost. Purchased with assistance from
Friends of the National-
museum in 1975.

Besides *The Oath of the Batavians*, the most significant paintings in the Netherlandish
collection are two works by Rubens: *Bacchanal in Andros* and *Worship of Venus*, copies
of paintings Titian executed for Isabella d'Este of Ferrara (now in Madrid). These
Rubens paintings were donated by King Karl XV when the current building was completed. No one knows how these two paintings came to Sweden. It seems most likely that
Karl XV's grandfather, the Napoleonic general Jean Baptiste Bernadotte, who became
Swedish King Karl XIV Johan, acquired them during a military campaign.

Seventeenth-century Netherlandish painting has continued to be cherished by Swedish
collectors in modern times. As a result, the museum has continuously been enriched by
purchases and donations in this area.

Görel Cavalli-Björkman

Jan van Hemessen
(Hemessen 1504 – Haarlem 1575)
Virgin and Child
Signed, dated 1544
Oil on panel, 145 × 101
NM 2140

Hemessen belonged to the so-called Romanists, who tried to unite Netherlandish naturalism with the classical ideal of Raphael and Michelangelo. This is very much in evidence in the depiction of the Christ Child's muscular body. Gift of E. Brodin in 1919.

Pieter Aertsen
(Amsterdam 1503 – Amsterdam 1575)
Christ and the Adulteress
Oil on canvas, 122 × 180
NM 2106

The foreground of this work is dominated by a view of a town square and a still life arrangement of fruit and vegetables. The painting's religious motif can be discerned in the background, and may have been the excuse for this magnificent painting. Gift of Prince Kondakov, St Petersburg, in 1918.

Jan Massys
(Antwerp 1509 – Antwerp ca. 1573)
Venus Cythereia
Signed, dated 1561
Oil on panel, 130 × 156
NM 507

This Italian-inspired, nude female figure holds a bouquet of carnations – flowers that were considered to have aphrodisiac properties. For this reason it is unclear whether she represents

Venus, goddess of love, or Flora, the flower nymph. A detailed and precise view of the city of Genoa is in the background. War booty acquired from Prague in 1648.

Frans Floris the Elder
(Antwerp 1519/20 – Antwerp 1570)
Feast of the Sea Gods
Signed, dated 1561
Oil on panel, 126 × 226
NM 430

Floris, like his Italian colleagues, looked to classical texts for inspiration, especially to Ovid's *Metamorphoses*. The subject here is probably the return of Theseus and his followers to

Athens from the Calydonian boar hunt. They were entertained en route by the river god Achelous and his nymphs. War booty acquired from Prague in 1648.

Lucas van Valckenborch
(ca. 1530 – Frankfurt 1597)
Double Portrait of an Elderly Couple
Dated ca. 1597
Oil on canvas, 131 × 182

Valckenborch had to leave his Roman Catholic home town of Mecheln, settling in Frankfurt, a free city for Protestant refugees. This may be a portrait of himself

and his wife. In the background there is a sculpture of Martin Luther. The foreground still life was painted by Georg Flegel. Purchased 1988.
NM 6836

Adriaen de Vries
(Haag ca. 1560 – Prague
1627)
Psyche Carried by Cupids
Bronze, height 187
NMSK 352

Adriaen de Vries, a student
of the Italian Renaissance
master sculptor Giovanni da
Bologna, shared his teacher's
ambition to create complicated figural groups. Here,
Psyche seems to float for-
wards, having succeeded in
taking some of the miracu-
lous beauty potion from Per-
sephone, queen of the
underworld. Gift of M. von
Wahrendorff in 1863.

Peter Paul Rubens
(Siegen 1577 – Antwerp 1640)
Susannah and the Elders
Signed, dated 1614
Oil on canvas, 66 × 51
NM 603

Rubens painted this subject numerous times; this is a relatively early version. It is painted with thinned pigments, which give the impression almost of enamel painting, particularly in the body of Susannah. Acquired from Queen Lovisa Ulrika in 1760.

Peter Paul Rubens
Bacchanal in Andros
Probably 1630s
Oil on canvas, 200 × 215
NM 600

This painting, a free copy of a Titian original, records how Bacchus transformed water on the island of Andros into wine, and how the inhabitants became inebriated. The story is based on a text written by the ancient author Philostratos, who described such a painting in a contemporary Neapolitan villa. Titian's formal classicism has been replaced here by a more lively Baroque style. Gift of Karl XV in 1865.

Frans Snyders
(Antwerp 1579 – Antwerp 1657)
Still Life with Fruit Bowl in a Niche
Signed
Oil on panel, 89 × 62
NM 640

Snyders became the great reviver of Flemish still life painting. He replaced the rustic market scenes of an earlier generation with elegant compositions of dazzling silver bowls and porcelain dishes, embellished with grapes and other exotic fruits from southern lands. Acquired from Gustav III in 1792.

Jan Fyt
(Antwerp 1611 – Antwerp 1661)
Large Still Life of Abundant Game
Signed, dated 1651
Oil on canvas, 183 × 214
NM 433

Fyt was Antwerp's great still life specialist, and he excelled in magnificent compositions like this one. Here, the artist proves his consummate skill in depicting animal skins and bird feathers. Acquired from Gustav III in 1779.

Osias Beert
(Antwerp ca. 1580 – Antwerp
1629)
Still Life with Cherries
Oil on panel, 31 × 41
NM 3331

It was through use of the old
masters' technique of layer-
ing thin glazes that Beert
rendered a modest subject at
once both realistic and time-
less. His treatment gives the
subject an almost mysterious
quality. Still life painting was
a genre specially associated
with Protestant circles in
France and Flanders. Gift of
Friends of the National-
museum in 1939.

Jacob Jordaens
(Antwerp 1593 – Antwerp
1678)
*King Candaules of Lydia
Showing His Consort to
Gyges*
Dated ca. 1645
Oil on canvas, 193 × 157
NM 1159

Jordaens, like Rubens, came
from Antwerp, but was less
aristocratic in his preten-
sions. This picture has a
treacherous, positive quality.
The queen felt so violated by
her husband that she per-
suaded Gyges to murder
him. Shortly afterwards,
Gyges assumed the Lydian
throne himself. Gift of Axel
Bielke in 1872.

Anthony van Dyck
(Antwerp 1599 – London
1641)
Saint Jerome
Signed
Oil on canvas, 167 × 154
NM 404

Van Dyck was Rubens' most
gifted pupil and was, like his
mentor, extremely cosmo-
politan. Saint Jerome was a
subject to which he returned
several times, primarily in
the 1610s. Another version of
this composition is in the
Museum Boymans-van Beun-
ingen in Rotterdam. Pur-
chased from King Adolf
Fredrik in 1771.

Ambrosius Bosschaert the Elder
(Antwerp 1568 – Den Haag 1621)
Still Life with Large Flower Vase
Signed, dated 1620
Oil on panel, 129 × 85
NM 373

Seventeenth-century flower still lifes combined contemporary interest in the most beautiful flowers known at the time with a concern for realistic depiction. However, the subject represented was, in fact, far from realistic, since often the flowers depicted did not bloom at the same time. Acquired from Gustav III in 1792.

Frans Hals
(Antwerp 1580/81 – Haarlem
1666)
Daniel van Aken
Oil on canvas, 67 × 57
NM 1567

Frans Hals worked in Haarlem, and specialised in portraiture. He painted his
associates without flattery
and with a strong sense of
their individuality. Pur-
chased 1901.

Hendrik Terbrugghen
(Deventer 1587 – Utrecht
1629)
Boy Playing the Lute
Oil on canvas, 103 × 84
NM 1487

Hendrik Terbrugghen
belonged to the last generation of Netherlandish artists
who journeyed to Rome. His
style is a personal interpre-
tation of Caravaggio's, whose
innovations he incorporated
in his northern motifs. This
painting, representing hear-
ing, probably belonged to a
series depicting the five
senses. Purchased 1895.

Rembrandt Harmensz. van Rijn
(Leyden 1606 – Amsterdam 1669)
The Kitchen Maid
Signed, dated 1651
Oil on canvas, 78 × 63
NM 584

This painting is considered one of the most representative of Rembrandt's works from the 1650s. It is painted with broad brushstrokes and built up with a rich impasto. The motif belongs to a series executed between 1645 and 1655, all of which straddle the boundary between portraiture and genre. Purchased by Gustav III, acquired by the museum in 1792.

Rembrandt Harmensz. van Rijn
The Oath of the Batavians to Claudius Civilis
Dated 1661–62
Oil on canvas, 196 × 309
NM 578

This painting was commissioned for the Amsterdam city hall. It did not, however, meet the city fathers' expectations, and was returned to the artist. Only the central part survives. The subject, which comes from Tacitus, concerns the Batavians' rebellion against the Romans, a tale considered to be parallel to the contemporary Dutch fight for independence from Spain. The painting was donated to the Academy of Art in the eighteenth century. Deposited at the Nationalmuseum in 1864.

Rembrandt Harmensz. van Rijn
The Oath of the Batavians to Claudius Civilis, detail
1661–62

The free brushwork in Rembrandt's late paintings is very clear in the depiction of the glass on the right hand side of the Claudius painting.

Rembrandt Harmensz. van Rijn
Simeon in the Temple
Dated 1669
Oil on canvas, 98 × 79
NM 4567

This painting was probably left unfinished on Rembrandt's easel at the time of his death. The artist has distilled his subject to the meeting between the Christ child and the God-fearing Simeon who, according to a revelation, would not die until he had beheld the Lord's anointed one. Gift of Nils B. Hersloff in 1949.

Rembrandt Harmensz. van Rijn
Sleeping Woman by a Window
Pen, brush and wash, 16.3 × 17.5
NMH 2084/1863

This drawing, executed with a broad reed pen and a brush, can be compared with Rembrandt's paintings of maids by windows, such as the Nationalmuseum's *The Kitchen Maid* from 1651. Purchased by C. G. Tessin from the art dealer Crozat in Paris.

Judith Leyster
(Haarlem 1609 – Heemstede
1660)
Boy Playing the Flute
Signed, dated 1630s
Oil on canvas, 73 × 62
NM 3384

This painting, one of the
artist's most important, was
painted in the early 1630s. Its
subject combines a genre
scene with still life and portraiture. Gift of King Oscar
II in 1871.

Isaac van Ostade
(Haarlem 1621 – Haarlem 1649)
Self Portrait
Signed, dated 1641
Oil on panel, 26 × 23
NM 557

Like his brother Adriaen, Isaac van Ostade specialised in peasant interiors. In recent times this portrait has been considered a self portrait, painted when the artist was twenty years old. Acquired from Queen Lovisa Ulrika in 1760.

Constantin Verhout
(Worked in Gouda during the 1660s)
Sleeping Student
Signed, dated 1663
Oil on panel, 38 × 31
NM 677

Verhout is a little-known artist. While the subject of the painting is, ostensibly, a sleeping student, the still life in the foreground is the artistic focus of the work. Its purpose is probably a moral one, reminding the viewer about the transience of life, and the importance of using one's time on earth appropriately. Acquired from C. G. Tessin in 1749.

Allart van Everdingen
(Alkmaar 1621 – Amsterdam 1675)
Landscape with Waterfall
Dated ca. 1644
Oil on canvas, 119 × 114
NM 2087

Van Everdingen visited Sweden and Norway in 1644. He was especially captivated by the forests, waterfalls and fjords – features which, for a Dutchman, must have been an exotic experience. This painting was executed in Scandinavia. Gift of Axel Beskow in 1918.

Karel Dujardin
(Amsterdam 1622 – Venice 1678)
Peasant Girl Milking a Cow
Signed
Oil on canvas, 66 × 59
NM 485

Dujardin studied in Italy, and his painting combines the restraint of the classical tradition with a realistic flavour of daily life. Acquired from Queen Lovisa Ulrika in 1760.

Jan van de Cappelle
(Amsterdam 1625/26 – Amsterdam 1679)
Harbour Scene with Reflecting Water
Signed, dated 1649
Oil on panel, 55 × 70
NM 562

For obvious reasons, seascapes were natural subjects for Dutch painters. Van de Cappelle concentrated on the pictorial possibilities of the foreground's tranquil water in this, his first signed painting. Acquired from King Adolf Fredrik in 1771.

Jacob van Ruisdael
(Haarlem 1628/29 – Amsterdam 1682)
View of Egmont
Oil on panel, 31 × 35
NM 618

Ruisdael is considered Holland's foremost landscape painter. Here, a high horizon dominates a spacious landscape, whose expanse is reflected in the shadows of clouds that enliven the plain in front of the town's silhouette. Acquired from C. G. Tessin in 1749.

Pieter de Hooch
(Rotterdam 1629 – Amsterdam 1683)
Interior with a Young Lady Reading
Probably late 1660s
Oil on canvas, 57 × 48
NM 471

This painting depicts a common subject in Dutch painting: a young woman absorbed in reading, or in writing, a love letter. Acquired from Queen Lovisa Ulrika in 1760.

Willem van Aelst
(Delft 1625/26 – Amsterdam 1683)
Still Life with Hunting Gear
Signed, dated 1664
Oil on canvas, 68 × 54
NM 301

Van Aelst worked in France from 1645 to 1649, and in Italy until 1656. His Dutch training is revealed in his masterly description of detail, while the cool colours and stiff composition betray the influence of his southern European colleagues. Purchased by Gustav III, acquired by the museum in 1792.

Melchior d'Hondecoeter
(Utrecht 1636 – Amsterdam 1695)
Still Life with Birds and Hunting Gear
Signed
Oil on panel, 56 × 46
NM 467

d'Hondecoeter specialised in depicting birds. Here, he chose to represent a game bag in a severe composition with restrained colours. Acquired from C. G. Tessin in 1749.

Vincent van Gogh
(Zundert 1853 – Auvers-sur-Oise 1890)
Acacia in Flower
Dated 1890
Oil on canvas, 33 × 24
NM 5939

This painting was executed during the last year of the artist's life. Its subject is taken from the garden of Paul Gachet, his doctor in Auvers. Despite a lapse of centuries, the rendering of acacia trees is strongly reminiscent of the Dutch still life tradition. Purchased in 1966.

chapter 7   Russia – Icons

In 1933, the Nationalmuseum acquired a collection of 245 icons, most of which were Russian, and thereupon became an international leader in this field. The donor was the Swedish banker Olof Aschberg (1877–1960). He had resided in Moscow on and off during the 1920s, where his interest in icons – and his collection – began; the majority of those he gave to the museum were acquired at this time. Following the 1933 gift, Aschberg continued to collect and, in 1952, donated an additional thirty or so icons.

Prior to 1933, the museum had few icons. Among them was one, however, that is still a cornerstone of the collection: a fourteenth-century Byzantine icon of *Christ Pantocrator* (110 × 66, NMI 276). It was acquired in 1917 from the Danish archaeologist and draughtsman Halvor Bagge, one of the earliest collectors of Byzantine art and icons in Scandinavia. This icon attracted great attention when it was shown at the European Council's 'Byzantine Art' exhibition in Athens in 1964.

The collection's oldest Russian material, also dating from the fourteenth century, is comprised of two icons, *The Apostle Peter* and *A Female Martyred Saint*, (each 73 × 24.5, NMI 294–295) and originally parts of the same work. The red background colour, for instance, identifies these as works belonging to the Novgorod school, a key centre in medieval Russia, and well represented in the collection.

Of the total number of icons, more than 300, about a quarter are Russian works dating from before 1700. The rest of the collection is comprised of later Russian icons and a small number from Greece and the Balkans, mostly dating from the eighteenth and nineteenth centuries.

Icons, the holy images of the Orthodox church, developed a formal language that differs greatly from the western European Renaissance ideal. Their severe stylisation, two-dimensional handling, gold background and general character emphasise the fact that they belong to a different dimension, distinct from the reality of the everyday. It is here that heavenly, not earthly, truth reigns. At the same time, this formal, abstract aspect of icons became a significant source of inspiration for twentieth-century modernism, in Russia as well as in western Europe and the United States.

Ulf Abel

Dormition of the Mother of God, section

The Holy Friday
Russian icon, sixteenth century, Novgorod school
Tempera on panel. 67.5 × 54
NMI 246

The saint is shown here bearing a cross and a caption with the first words of the Nicene Creed. It was with these that she endured her martyrdom. Her mantle is blood red, but her headcloth is white, a symbol of virginity. Gift of Olof Aschberg in 1952.

The Holy Nicholas with Scenes from His Life
Russian icon, sixteenth century, central Russia
Tempera on panel, 92 × 70
NMI 272

The Holy Nicholas, the bishop of Myra during the fourth century, is represented in the centre, wearing his bishop's robes, distinguished by a cross pattern. The surrounding scenes illustrate his life from birth (upper left), to death and burial (lower right). Here the artist shows, among other scenes, the saint as the protector of sailors. Gift of Olof Aschberg in 1952.

Dormition of the Mother of God
Russian icon, sixteenth century
Tempera on panel, 67 × 49
NMI 248

The apostles, bishops and mourning women are gathered around the death-bed of Mary, while Christ is ready to convey her soul, in the form of an infant, to heaven. Christ is surrounded by candle-bearing angels, four-winged cherubs, and a six-winged seraph. Gift of Olof Aschberg in 1952.

The Holy George
Russian icon, sixteenth
century
Tempera on panel, 94 × 66.5
NMI 191

Saint George's battle with the
dragon, symbolising the fight
between good and evil, is
here transformed into a
ritualistic, rhythmic dance,
or a cultish game. Gift of
Olof Aschberg in 1933.

*Processional Icon with the
Fiery Ascension of the
Prophet Elijah*
Russian icon, sixteenth cen-
tury, Novgorod school
Tempera on panel,
56.5 × 54.5; height with staff,
110.5
NMI 314

The subject of this processional icon – whose front
depicts Novgorod's protec-
tion image, the so-called
'God's Mother of the Sign'
as well as its style, identify it
as a work of the Novgorod
school. The rim figures represent the saints Nicholas
and Vlasy. Acquired 1990.

The Meeting of Joachim and Anna
Russian icon, seventeenth century
Tempera on panel, 106.5 × 73
NMI 273

The Apochrypha tell how Mary's parents were separately informed by angels that, in spite of their age, they would be blessed with a daughter. They then met in a tender embrace before the Golden Gate, one of the city gates of Jerusalem. Gift of Olof Aschberg in 1952.

chapter **8**   # Spain

The Spanish collection consists of a few works acquired in recent times. El Greco's *Apostles Peter and Paul* was purchased in 1935 for a price considered astronomical at the time. The acquisition of Zurbaran's painting *The Veil of Saint Veronica* twenty years later was an important complement to it, since it also possessed a unique character and represented an imaginative subject.

Since 1949, the Nationalmuseum has owned an outstanding portrait by Goya of his friend, the architect Ventura Rodriguez (NM 4574). In 1961 the museum had the opportunity to obtain two more works by the Spanish master, *Poetry and Poets* (NM 5592) and *Spain, Time and History* (NM 5593). At first it was not clear quite what a seminal work the latter was but, through the scholarship of Eleanor Sayres, it appears that this is a monument to Spain's first, fragile democracy and, therefore, a picture with important symbolic significance, even today.

Görel Cavalli-Björkman

Francisco Goya, *Spain, Time and History*, section

El Greco (born Domenikos Theotocopoulos)
(Crete 1541 – Toledo 1614)
The Apostles Peter and Paul
Dated 1596–1608
Oil on canvas, 124 × 93
NM 3077

The apostles Peter and Paul are a subject to which El Greco returned on at least three occasions between 1590 and 1608. Even though he used the same composition, the three versions are radically different. This one is thought to be the last, and most carefully worked, version. Purchased 1935.

Francisco de Zurbaran
(Fuente de Cantos 1598 –
Madrid 1664)
The Veil of Saint Veronica
Oil on canvas, 70 × 51.5
NM 5382

Zurbaran worked primarily
in Seville and concentrated
on religious paintings in the
mystical, spiritual style popu-
lar in Spain at the time. This
painting can be viewed as a
distillation of this style,
especially in its characteristic
opposition between the linen
cloth's illusionistic reality
and the face of Christ, which
appears as a vision. Pur-
chased 1957.

Louis Meléndez
(Naples 1716 – Madrid 1780)
*A Basket of Wild Straw-
berries in a Landscape*
Dated 1759–74
Oil on canvas, 36.5 × 59.5
NM 6869

This painting belongs to the
artist's later oeuvre, when he
abandoned traditional still
life compositions. The
objects appear as abstract
artefacts against a dark background. Here, Meléndez has
placed a basket of wild straw-
berries in their natural
environment, accompanied
by a landscape with dramatic
cloud formations. Purchased
1992.

Francisco Goya y Lucientes
(Fuendetodos 1746 –
Bordeaux 1828)
*Seated Woman and Man in
a Spanish Cloak*
Dated 1824
Miniature on ivory, 9 × 8.5
NMB 1879

This picture belongs to a
small group of miniatures
executed by Goya during his
exile in Bordeaux. In this
work he introduced a new
technique. He first blackened
the entire field, and then
developed his subject by

dropping water on it, letting
chance decide the forms that
emerged. The subject is close
to those found in the frescoes
he painted for his own house,
the *Quinta del Sordo* (House
of the Deaf Man). Purchased
1963.

Francisco Goya y Lucientes
(Fuendetodos 1746 –
Bordeaux 1828)
Spain, Time and History
Dated 1812
Oil on canvas, 294 × 244
NM 5593

This painting is a political allegory celebrating Spain's 1812 constitution, a document which contained liberal and radical ideas rooted in the French Revolution. The constitution was annulled two years later, the reactionaries triumphed, and by 1824 Goya felt compelled to go into exile. Gift of Friends of the Nationalmuseum in 1961.

chapter 9   Germany

The German collection has its origin in the Royal collection of the sixteenth century, a period when Sweden was in close contact with Germany. Gustav Vasa was the first Swedish Renaissance prince, and during his early years as regent he amassed for himself a sizeable art collection. According to an inventory of 1547, it comprised 92 objects, among which were paintings by Lucas Cranach the Elder (*Lucretia*, signed and dated 1528; NM 1080), and Lucas Cranach the Younger (*Christ and the Adulteress*, signed with the artist's signum, a winged snake; NM 253). Both paintings are now in the Nationalmuseum.

During the seventeenth century, the German collection was enriched by Swedish military expeditions on the Continent. In 1632, Swedish troops plundered the Elector of Munich's collection. In this way Sweden gained another painting by Cranach the Elder, *The Payment* (signed and dated 1532; NM 258), and several paintings by Ludwig Refinger and Abraham Schöpfer. When the Swedish army invaded Prague in 1648, Sweden acquired several more paintings by Cranach the Elder, as well as a painting by Hans Baldung Grien, *Mercury* (NM 1073).

Around 1900 the collection was strengthened with several paintings dating from the late nineteenth century. Works by Franz von Lenbach and Hans Thoma were purchased in connection with the 1897 International Art and Industry Exposition in Stockholm. In 1911, the museum acquired a painting by Max Liebermann (*Rider on the Beach*); three years later saw the most noteworthy acquisition from abroad in a portrait by Liebermann's contemporary Wilhelm Leibl, purchased at the Baltic Exhibition in Malmö.

German painting, represented by almost 100 works, plays a minor role in the museum's collection. A quarter of these date from the sixteenth century; the remainder is evenly distributed among succeeding centuries.

Cecilia Engellau-Gullander

Abraham Schöpfer, *Mucius Scaevola before King Porsenna*, detail

Albrecht Dürer
(Nürnberg 1471 – Nürnberg 1528)
Portrait of a Young Girl
Signed, dated 1515
Black crayon and soft brown
watercolour, 42.3 × 29.4
NMH 1855/1863

It has been suggested that
the model was Felicitas
Pirkheimer, who would have
been about 19 at the time.
She was newly engaged,
which may explain the
beautiful hairband. The
drawing belongs to a group
of monumental portraits of
people who are thought to
have been close friends and
family of Dürer. Purchased
from C. G. Tessin between
1741 and 1749.

Lucas Cranach the Elder
(Kronach 1472 – Weimar
1553)
The Payment
Signed, dated 1532
Oil on panel, 108 × 119
NM 258

The subject goes back to the
Netherlandish theme of the
ill-matched couple. It exemplifies two of the seven
deadly sins: lust in the old
man, and avarice in the
young woman. The pome-
granate (the fruit of love),
the linen fabric, and the flies
spoiling the cheese emphasise the two-fold character of
the transaction. This work
was once the property of the
Emperor Maximilian of
Bavaria. Acquired as war
booty from Munich in 1632.

Hans Baldung, called Grien
(Weyersheim 1484/85 –
Strasbourg 1545)
Mercury
Dated ca. 1530
Oil on panel, 194 × 64
NM 1073

This painting, representing
Mercury as the god of his
namesake planet, is a wing
panel from an astronomical
clock, once housed in Rudolf
II's collection in Prague. On
the inside are medallions of
Saturn and Mercury.
Another wing panel, *The
Creation of Humans and
Animals*, is in Erfurt. It was
previously part of Rudolf II's
collection. Acquired as war
booty by Sweden in 1648.

Abraham Schöpfer
(Birth/death details unknown)
Mucius Scaevola Before
King Porsenna
Signed, dated 1533
Oil on panel, 157 × 120
NM 295

The painting belongs to a
suite of eight cosmic 'world
landscapes' requested by
Wilhelm IV of Bavaria. In
the foreground is the impri-
soned Mucius Scaevola, a
hero in the war between the

Romans and Etruscans,
whose exploits are recorded
by the Roman historian Livy.
The only known autographed
and dated work by the artist.
Acquired as war booty from
Munich in 1632.

Max Liebermann
(Berlin 1847 – Berlin 1935)
Rider on the Beach
Signed, dated 1911
Oil on canvas, 70 × 100
NM 1729

Around the turn of the century, Liebermann began painting this subject in a number of versions. As time went on, his palette became lighter and the brushwork broader. In this version, the rider is recorded with Impressionistic elegance. The playful, jumping dog, and the waves breaking against the shore, strengthen the feeling of a momentary impression. Purchased 1911.

Index